standing firm in Christ

BIBLICAL PRINCIPLES FOR FIGHTING SPIRITUAL BATTLES

Therefore put on the full armor of God, so that when the day of evil comes, you may be able to stand your ground, and after you have done everything, to stand.

(Ephesians 6:13)

dianne thornton

Visit Dianne Thornton online at www.diannethornton.com

Standing Firm in Christ: Biblical Principles for Fighting Spiritual Battles

Copyright © 2020, by Dianne Thornton. All rights reserved.

Cover photo by Pexels (https://pixabay.com/users/pexels-2286921/) from Pixabay.

Cover photo adjustment by Kenzie McDonald (https://mysketchylife.net)

Edited by Suzy Taylor Oakley

No part of this publication may be reproduced, stored in a retrieval system, stored in a database and/or published in any form or by any means, electronic, mechanical, photocopying, recording, or otherwise, without the prior written permission of the publisher.

Library of Congress Control Number: 2020916149

All Scripture quotations, unless otherwise indicated, are taken from the Holy Bible, New International Version®, NIV®. Copyright ©1973, 1978, 1984, 2011 by Biblica Inc.™ Used by permission of Zondervan. All rights reserved worldwide. www.zondervan.com The "NIV" and "New International Version" are trademarks registered in the United States Patent and Trademark Office by Biblica Inc.™

Scripture quotations from the ESV® Bible (The Holy Bible, English Standard Version®), copyright © 2001 by Crossway, a publishing ministry of Good News Publishers. Used by permission. All rights reserved.

Scripture quotations marked CSB have been taken from the Christian Standard Bible®, Copyright © 2017 by Holman Bible Publishers. Used by permission. Christian Standard Bible® and CSB® are federally registered trademarks of Holman Bible Publishers.

Scripture quotations taken from the Amplified® Bible (AMP), Copyright © 2015 by The Lockman Foundation Used by permission. www.Lockman.org.

ISBN-13-978-0-578-69181-7

endorsements

I'll never forget the first time I heard the term "spiritual warfare." I had no idea what it was, and even less understanding what to do about it. **STANDING FIRM IN CHRIST: Biblical Principles for Fighting Spiritual Battles** *is exactly the kind of study I needed then, and that all believers need to know how to effectively war against our real enemy and win. God has already given us everything we need for life and godliness, but we need to know how to appropriate those weapons and implement them. Standing Firm in Christ brings Ephesians 6:10-20 to life for our practical everyday use. If more believers understood these Biblical principles, they would be living from a place of victory, rather than striving for victory.*

Dr. Michelle Bengtson, board certified neuropsychologist, international speaker, and author of three award-winning books, including: *Hope Prevails: Insights from a Doctor's Personal Journey Through Depression*; the *Hope Prevails Bible Study*; **and** *Breaking Anxiety's Grip: How to Reclaim the Peace God Promises*

There has never been a day when we need to stand tall as Christians as there is right now! And, author Dianne Thornton has provided a timely tool to encourage us and help us to make that stand. Packed with Bible truths, practical experiences, and words of wisdom, this Bible study is perfect for the season we are living in today. I highly recommend that you grab a copy of **STANDING FIRM IN CHRIST**.

Melanie Redd, author of *Live in Light: 5-Minute Devotions for Teen Girls*

This is not just a simple armory, but a training ground and a close look into the heart of the Lord of Hosts. Dianne masterfully teaches us how to practically wear our armor, while leaning into Christ, who is the fulfillment of each piece. He is our truth, peace, and victory! I am so excited to share this study with my friends.

Stefani Stoltzfus, Founder of Warrior Hearted Mom

*Prepare to have your spirit strengthened, your faith bolstered, and your biblical understanding of Christian living deepened as you embark on this journey with Dianne Thornton, **STANDING FIRM IN CHRIST: Biblical Principles for Fighting Spiritual Battles**. With her inimitable style of story-sharing, humility, and humor, Dianne delves right into the key truths of the Christian's armor, and how the Lord, Himself, is our victory. This is a serious study of the scriptures, complete with a sound use of the Bible's original languages and theological insights but written in such a practical and easy-to-read fashion that you will easily grasp and interact with each principle. And for anyone who engages in the applicational features of this journey, I strongly believe there will be spiritual growth in meeting life's challenges! Fasten your seatbelt!*

Gary L. Hauck, ThM, DMin, PhD

This is a must-read for anyone who wants to strengthen their faith so they can stand firm in the face of life's trials. Diane doesn't just tell you what you need to know, she teaches you how to study Scripture for yourself. This is truly a Bible study for such a time as this.

Misty Phillip, author of *The Struggle is Real: But So is God* **and host of "By His Grace" podcast**

I heard this statement once, and it "stuck" like glue in my brain. The pastor stated, "we need to get people into God's Word, then, God's Word will get into people!" Dianne Thornton is a Word-saturated woman. All you have to do to know that is to be around her! Even better than knowing her, is being able to "virtually" hang out with her through her study, ***STANDING FIRM IN CHRIST: Biblical Principles for Fighting Spiritual Battles***. *As you read, you can easily imagine having a conversation across the table with her. Dianne wants to see God's Word transform our world. She has done a huge part in that desire being fulfilled with this 8-week study on how we fight (and win) the numerous spiritual battles that come our way. Pick it up, and get ready for an amazing, life-changing ride!*

Jason Hess, executive pastor, Redemption Church, Pearland, Texas

If there's one thing I know about Dianne Thornton, it's that she desires to rightly divide the Word of Truth and earnestly seeks to explain it in a way her audience can understand–and not only understand, but practically apply. This book thoroughly explains the how and why of the importance of putting on the full armor of God. It walks the reader carefully through each piece of armor, how it relates to specific names of God, the enemy's tactics against each piece, and how to personally strategize an action plan. Drawing from the original Greek and Hebrew root words, the book delves deeply into definitions and terms the reader must know to fully grasp the meaning of clothing oneself with God's armor. While the book explains this concept in depth, it remains practical and full of stories that relate to daily life, keeping the reader's interest while endearing the writer even more. The journaling pages are purposefully crafted with specific questions to prompt reader answers. I can't wait for this book to be in print!!!

Ruthie Gray, podcast host of *Instagram Insider Hacks*

for the One who makes us stand firm

contents

endorsements iii

supplemental materials x

acknowledgements xi

preface xiv

introduction xvi

ephesians 6:10-20 xxii

week one – preparing for battle 1

    WEEKLY PREP 2

    FIGHTING IN GOD'S STRENGTH 3

    OUR ENEMY 13

    TAKE YOUR STAND 17

    IN CHRIST 21

    PERSONAL ACTION PLAN 25

week two – the sword of the Spirit 27

    WEEKLY PREP 28

    THE WORD OF GOD 29

    THE SWORD OF THE SPIRIT 37

    THE ENEMY OF THE WORD OF GOD 41

    STANDING FIRM WITH THE SWORD OF THE SPIRIT 45

    PERSONAL ACTION PLAN 49

week three – powerful prayer 51

 WEEKLY PREP 52

 PRAYER THAT MAKES A DIFFERENCE 53

 HOW WE PRAY 57

 THE ENEMY OF PRAYER 61

 STANDING FIRM IN PRAYER 65

 PERSONAL ACTION PLAN 69

week four – the belt of truth 71

 WEEKLY PREP 72

 THE GOD OF TRUTH 73

 THE BELT OF TRUTH 79

 OUR ENEMY IS A LIAR 83

 STANDING FIRM IN THE TRUTH 87

 PERSONAL ACTION PLAN 91

week five – the breastplate of righteousness 93

 WEEKLY PREP 94

 THE GOD OF RIGHTEOUSNESS 95

 THE BREASTPLATE OF RIGHTEOUSNESS 103

 OUR ENEMY EXPLOITS OUR WEAKNESSES 109

 STANDING FIRM IN CHRIST'S RIGHTEOUSNESS 113

 PERSONAL ACTION PLAN 117

week six – the gospel of peace 119

 WEEKLY PREP 120

 THE GOD OF PEACE 121

 THE FIRM FOUNDATION OF THE GOSPEL OF PEACE 127

 THE ENEMY OF THE GOSPEL OF PEACE 131

 STANDING FIRM WITH THE PRINCE OF PEACE 137

 PERSONAL ACTION PLAN 141

week seven – the shield of faith **143**

- WEEKLY PREP 144
- OUR FAITHFUL GOD 145
- THE SHIELD OF FAITH 153
- OUR ENEMY'S FLAMING ARROWS 157
- STANDING FIRM IN OUR GOD'S FAITHFULNESS 161
- PERSONAL ACTION PLAN 165

week eight – the helmet of salvation **167**

- WEEKLY PREP 168
- OUR VICTORIOUS, SAVING GOD 169
- THE HELMET OF SALVATION 177
- THE ENEMY WANTS TO CONTROL OUR MINDS 181
- STANDING FIRM IN VICTORY WITH THE MIND OF CHRIST 185
- PERSONAL ACTION PLAN 191
- IN CONCLUSION 193

appendix **197**

- HOW TO USE BIBLEGATEWAY 199
- HOW TO STUDY ONE VERSE 202
- MEET JESUS! 208
- ABOUT THE AUTHOR 210
- ENDNOTES 211

supplemental materials

The following digital downloads are available to enhance your study of STANDING FIRM IN CHRIST: Biblical Principles for Fighting Spiritual Battles: https://diannethornton.com/shop

Standing Firm in Christ–Leader Guide (22 pages)

Group discussion is one way to deepen personal learning. The leader guide provides facilitators guidance for this 8-week Bible study. This guide identifies key questions and the key truths for each week to ensure members understand the essential truths for each week. Tips for leading a small group effectively are also included

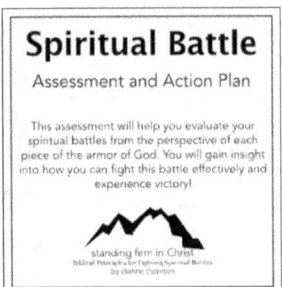

Spiritual Battle Assessment and Action Plan (8 pages)

This assessment takes a deep dive into a spiritual battle from the perspective of each piece of the armor of God. Targeted journaling questions help you gain insight into your battle so you can stand firm against your enemy and experience victory!

Scripture Memory Cards Bundle

Hide God's Word in your heart with this set of Scripture memory cards for Ephesians 6:10-20. Cards include both NIV and ESV. Blank cards can be used for additional verses you want to memorize or for keeping track of prayer requests.

acknowledgements

This project would not have made it to completion without the support of many friends and family members. My typical approach to a project is to dive in and not come up for air until it's finished. This project, however, did not go that way. I was distracted by "mom" commitments and "anything but writing" activities. Although I felt strongly about God's call to get this message out, the delays made me feel as though I had missed the window for its effectiveness. But God's ways are not our ways. His timing is not our timing.

Tim–You are my strongest supporter. You encouraged me all along the way and consistently insisted I complete this project. Sometimes you encouraged me to get away from the familiar so I wouldn't be distracted. Your wisdom and insight gave me food for thought as I worked through difficult concepts. Thanks for not getting upset when I had no plans for dinner. You jumped in and made sure we had something tasty to eat.

Max, Rachel, and Abby–Watching you become young adults has been the joy of my life, especially as you encouraged me with godly wisdom. When I felt discouraged, you reminded me that people were waiting for these words "with my voice." You often asked, "How's your Bible study coming?" For a long time, I couldn't say that I'd made great progress! But I was excited when I had worked hard to give you something to review.

Mom, Dad, and Claudia–Y'all are my best cheerleaders! You always lift my spirits.

Peggi–Your challenge to write better and dig deeper made a difference.

Gary–Thank you for ensuring I used original languages properly!

My church family–Thank you for trusting me with your ladies.

Suzy–Thank you for being patient with me as we worked through editing this project. Your attention to detail and style have made this book easy to read!

Tammy–Thank you for evaluating my content–and risking our friendship to speak truth. Your honest words make me and my writing better and more effective. (And that subtitle!!!) You are iron!

My pilot Bible study ladies–Bea, Bev, Carmel, Carole, Claudia, Daniella, Georgia, Jeannine, Jennifer, Julia, Linda, Lynn, Sheri, Tammy, Teddy, Toni, your feedback helped to make this study understandable and better for those who follow you. Thanks for putting up with all my "asks" in the group chat and my last-minute changes! You are amazing!

Jesus–You are my best friend. You are present when others aren't. You understand when others don't. You alone have the power to change. Thank You for helping me stand firm in my own struggles, for picking me up when I fall, and enabling me to stand firm again. I love you.

preface

Four years ago, I led the opening sessions for the women's Bible study at my church, which included sharing a brief devotional. Sometimes I recruited others to share what God was doing in their lives. Other times, I read from one of my well-loved devotional books. Occasionally, I shared what God had shown me in my quiet times.

In the early part of 2016, my Facebook feed was filled with articles about the armor of God. I was turned off by it. All of it. I scrolled past every post.

I grew up in a Christian family with parents who taught me to love God's Word. "Praying on the armor" was (and still is) a regular part of my mom's prayer life. But somehow, it didn't hold meaning for me. To me, praying through a litany of verses was just "one more thing" to do in my quiet time. *I know. I shouldn't feel that way, right?* But it overwhelmed me. When I saw all these posts in my feed, I felt frustration and guilt. And that's exactly where the enemy wanted me. Immobile and ineffective.

Toward the end of that school year, the Lord prompted me to take my own look at Ephesians 6:10-20 and not worry about what everyone else wrote, but to read it for what *He* wanted to show me. That's all. So I did.

What God showed me astounded me and gave me great freedom and hope! I learned that putting on the armor of God isn't so much about a prayer (although prayer is an essential weapon in the believer's arsenal) as it is about *who we are in Christ*. Yes, we have a role in this. But God is the One who molds us into Christ's image. And this is how we fight our enemy.

I was so excited! After sharing this with the ladies at my church, the educational director for our women's ministry told me that if I was going to write another Bible study, it should be on this topic. She sensed that women needed this message. **Standing Firm in Christ**: *Biblical Principles for Fighting Spiritual Battles* was born.

It would be another four years, however, before I finished writing it. I started this study during my kids' high school years, and they were busy. I was involved in their activities and made those my priority. After they graduated, my husband was laid off, so I began substitute teaching to provide a little income. Throughout those years, I wrote on and off. By the time COVID-19 entered, the study was about half-way complete. Because the virus halted all other activities, I sat down and finally finished what I started.

The study you hold in your hands is not the same as the one I began writing in 2016. The title has changed; the approach has changed. But the message is the same, and one our world needs today! Our enemy fights to keep souls from finding Jesus and to keep Christians ineffective. He even stirs up strife within the Christian community.

We need to recognize his tactics and stand firm amid the fight. ***Standing Firm in Christ****: Biblical Principles for Fighting Spiritual Battles* will show you how to do that.

introduction

Once during my weekly chores, I forgot to take paper towels upstairs to clean my bathroom mirror. I intended to take care of it later, but I forgot. As the following week wore on, my mirror continued to collect toothpaste splatter, extra-hold hair spray, dust, and who knows what else. All of that obscured the reflection of anyone who looked in the mirror. What a difference it made when I finally cleaned it! The next time I got ready for the day, I was able to see myself clearly.

God's plan for believers is for us to be conformed to the image of His Son (Romans 8:29). He wants us to become like Christ in the ways we think, speak, and act. When we develop His attitudes and characteristics, we reflect Him accurately. But how is that possible?

God wants us to know Him. He wants us to seek Him. He promises that when we seek Him, we will find Him (Jeremiah 29:13-14). Throughout Scripture, God introduced Himself to the Israelites a little at a time. As He revealed a new aspect of His character, either He or they gave Him a new name to describe it. Jesus is the physical embodiment of what we know about God. He made His home on earth so we could know Him. God is sovereign; Jesus is sovereign. God is ruler; Jesus is ruler.

As we study all the pieces of God's armor, we will compare them to the attributes of God and how they are fulfilled in Jesus Christ. Then we will see how we stand firm in these truths. Each attribute of God that we will study is at the core of His being. He is fully true. He is completely righteous. He is peace. When we get a better view of God, we have a better view of ourselves. God is true; we are not. God is righteous; we are not. God is peace; we are not. That's why we need His armor. It's not the "Believer's armor," although it is given to us to wear. It is His character we put on. It is His character that allows us to stand firm against our enemy.

The Apostle Paul wrote his letter to the church in Ephesus while he was a prisoner (Ephesians 3:1, 4:1, and 6:20). Although it is not known exactly where he was imprisoned, most agree he was in Rome. Ephesus was a major city in the Asian region of the Roman Empire. Today, the excavated, ancient city of Ephesus is within the city of Selcuk, which is in the Province of Izmir, Turkey.

My children can tell you that, like most teachers, I take advantage of every opportunity to provide life lessons, turning the daily mundane into teachable moments. I think that's what Paul did when he wrote Ephesians 6:10-18.

I imagine him sitting in his quarters, observing the Roman centurion assigned to him. As he finished up the letter to the Ephesian church, he began paying closer attention to how the soldier was dressed and what he was wearing. Then God inspired him to write what we will now study.

APPROACH

The first three weeks cover the weapons of our warfare, while the following five weeks explore the armor of God.

Day 1 is a general discussion of the week's topic and will, for most days, include the study of a Name of God from the Old Testament. Day 1 sets the stage for the rest of the week.

Days 2-4 are personal study that will help you understand how the enemy attacks us and how we stand firm against him.

Day 5 includes guided journaling pages for your Personal Action Plan to help you apply what you learned earlier in the week. The battlefield prayers you write during this study will be specific to your current needs. Return to these pages and write new battlefield prayers as needed. For laser focus on a particular spiritual battle, a spiritual battle plan assessment kit is available in the shop on my website.

Using our offensive weapons in concert with God's armor will make us more effective in standing firm against our enemy.

In case you are like me and enjoy examining topics on a deeper level, I have provided opportunities to do so with BibleGateway, an online Bible study website. Occasionally I will dig into the original language a bit. Although I am not an expert, I have learned to use some handy tools and will share them with you.

If you were to pick any Hebrew word and look at its translation, you would see that one Hebrew word can be translated into different English words. In the same way, different Hebrew words are often translated into one English word. Today many resources are available to give us a better understanding of the original translation of God's Word.

Strong's Lexicon is a dictionary written especially for the Hebrew and Greek words in the Bible. It's readily available for free on many Bible study websites. Below are a few:

- In two places at Blue Letter Bible. You can select "Strong's" in the display options. It will insert the Strong's numeric identifier next to each word in a verse. Also, in the Interlinear (www.blueletterbible.org).

- In the Interlinear at Bible Hub (www.biblehub.com)

- Under **Our Library** / **Concordances** at Bible Study Tools (www.biblestudytools.com)

GETTING THE MOST OUT OF THE PERSONAL ACTION PLAN

Day 5 is your Personal Action Plan. This is your opportunity for deep, personal reflection and application. The day begins with one or two questions that ask where you are vulnerable to Satan's attacks (or lies) in the areas we studied that week. Next, you identify Scriptures that counter these lies and rewrite them into a battlefield prayer. The day ends with asking you to list any songs that encourage your heart for your specific situation.

For the Personal Action Plan to be effective, you need specific Bible verses that counter Satan's lies and speak truth to your needs. Below are several ways to discover them.

- Basic Google searches work well for finding lists of verses on a specific topic. The key is to include the words "Bible verses" in your search. For example, if you want to find verses related to worry, type "Bible verses for worry" in the search bar.

- Most Bibles have a concordance in the back. Concordances are arranged in alphabetical order. Look up a word related to your topic, and if that word is used in a Bible verse, the most popular uses are listed.

- You can also use cross-references (the superscripted letters within a Bible verse). If you know one verse, cross-references will lead you to other verses. If your Bible doesn't have cross-references, you can use BibleGateway's.

- The topical search on BibleGateway is another resource. Refer to the appendix to learn how to use BibleGateway.

WHAT ARE YOU WEARING?

When our children are tiny, we don't leave them alone in a room–even if we have done everything we know to childproof it. They need our watch care. Even though we created a safe space for them, tiny hands and fingers still seem to find their way into dangerous places.

As they get a little older, we extend their boundaries. We might leave them alone in a room, but we wouldn't dream of leaving them alone in the house. They are not mature enough to handle the "what ifs" of being alone. Plus, most of the time they would be frightened if left alone. Eventually, however, they mature and need to stretch their wings a bit to grow in independence.

When I used to run, I would leave my children alone for short time periods–like ten minutes–while I ran up and down our street. Over time, I stretched it out until I could get my entire run in and feel confident they were OK at home.

By the time they were teenagers, it was a joy knowing I could leave them home alone. They gained responsibility and earned my trust. I remember leaving the house before they did and saying (as I walked out the door), "Don't forget to lock up. And remember to set the alarm!"

When I got back home, the door was locked. When I unlocked and opened it, the alarm's warning system alerted me to punch in our code. They hadn't left the house unprotected!

Before Paul signs off his letter to the Ephesian church, he leaves them with parting words as well: a reminder to become strong in the Lord and to protect themselves with God's armor (Ephesians 6:10-11). Let's look closely at verses 11 and 13. They are almost the same. If Paul repeated this, we should pay close attention.

Verse 11	Verse 13
Put on the full armor of God	Therefore, put on the full armor of God
So	So
You can take your stand against	You may be able to stand your ground
The devil's schemes	When the day of evil comes
	And after you have done everything, to stand

Did you know that Paul uses the phrase "put on" or "clothe yourselves" in almost every book he wrote? In each instance, it is a metaphor describing the life and character of the believer. It's a reminder to live the way God calls us to live.

> *The night is nearly over; the day is almost here. So let us **put aside** the deeds of darkness and put on the armor of light. Let us behave decently, as in the daytime ... **clothe** yourselves with the Lord Jesus Christ, and do not think about how to gratify the desires of the flesh.* (Romans 13:12-14, emphasis added)

In these verses, Paul compares "deeds of darkness" to "dirty clothes" and "right living" to the "armor of light." We remove our dirty clothes and put on the clean clothes of right living as though it were midday with nothing to hide. Because we belong to Christ, we no longer think about ways to satisfy our flesh. Instead, because Jesus Christ lives in us, our lives should reflect His character. This is what Paul means when he says, "Clothe yourselves with Christ."

When Paul says to put on every piece of God's armor, he uses the warfare term, ***panoplia***–which is where our English word *panoply* comes from. This Greek word means "complete armor, offensive and defensive." Our English word means "a complete suit of armor." [1] In the same way a Roman soldier would not go into battle without his panoply of armor, Paul wants us to be completely prepared to face our enemy. And we need it!

The word *so* gives us the reason we need the armor of God: so we can stand against our enemy and his schemes.

Many people think of the armor of God as a mental checklist–consciously praying something like, "Lord, today I wear the belt of truth around my waist and Your righteousness as my breastplate," working their way through each piece until they are "fully armed."

Does praying a prayer like this truly prepare us for the battles we will surely face? I don't think so. In putting on the armor of God, Paul extends his metaphor for Christian living. Yes, it is purposeful, but it is not a magical prayer that assures readiness for battle when we "pray it" like this.

Throughout this study, we will learn how each piece of armor represents an aspect of Christ's character and how we reflect it in our lives. If we aren't wearing ALL of God's armor, we leave portions of our body exposed and vulnerable to Satan. We need ALL of God's armor to stand against ALL the strategies of the devil. God's armor provides EVERYTHING we need to stand against our enemy and experience victory.

A Note About Worship

2 Chronicles 20 tells the story of Judah's battle with Moab and Ammon. These two nations combined had a massive army. Outside of a miracle, there was no way Judah could defeat them. King

Jehoshaphat, along with the people of Judah, stood before the Lord and asked for His guidance. The beginning of his prayer is six long verses of worship! God's messenger, Jahaziel, encouraged Jehoshaphat not to be discouraged or afraid. He and his army were to stand firm and watch the Lord deliver them.

Early the next morning, Jehoshaphat appointed a team of worshipers to lead his army into battle. As they began to sing and praise, the Lord set ambushes against their enemies, and they destroyed one another.

Worship can be a powerful weapon in our battle against Satan. Whether we worship in song or recount the character qualities of the Lord, worship transforms our mindset. So prepared, we are better equipped to stand firm against our enemy and experience victory!

Part of your Personal Action Plan each week will be to develop the habit of worship in battle. A section is provided for you to list songs that help you apply the lessons you learned. By the time you've finished this study, you'll have a playlist that will keep your mind focused on the Lord and your heart at peace for your spiritual battles.

ephesians 6:10-20

¹⁰ Finally, be strong in the Lord and in his mighty power.

¹¹ Put on the full armor of God, so that you can take your stand against the devil's schemes.

¹² For our struggle is not against flesh and blood, but against the rulers, against the authorities, against the powers of this dark world and against the spiritual forces of evil in the heavenly realms.

¹³ Therefore put on the full armor of God, so that when the day of evil comes, you may be able to stand your ground, and after you have done everything, to stand.

¹⁴ Stand firm then, with the belt of truth buckled around your waist, with the breastplate of righteousness in place,

¹⁵ and with your feet fitted with the readiness that comes from the gospel of peace.

¹⁶ In addition to all this, take up the shield of faith, with which you can extinguish all the flaming arrows of the evil one.

¹⁷ Take the helmet of salvation and the sword of the Spirit, which is the word of God.

¹⁸ And pray in the Spirit on all occasions with all kinds of prayers and requests. With this in mind, be alert and always keep on praying for all the Lord's people.

¹⁹ Pray also for me, that whenever I speak, words may be given me so that I will fearlessly make known the mystery of the gospel,

²⁰ for which I am an ambassador in chains. Pray that I may declare it fearlessly, as I should.

week one – preparing for battle

day 1 – fighting in God's strength

day 2 – our enemy

day 3 – take your stand

day 4 – in Christ

day 5 – personal action plan

week 1 | standing firm in Christ

weekly prep

What is your current battle? It doesn't have to be a big thing, although it may be. If it is a big thing, you know exactly what it is. You may be walking through intense suffering. The Holy Spirit may have His finger on an area in your life you don't want to change. Perhaps you are working through a life-style change–and it's hard!

If something doesn't come to mind, think about what is bugging you today. Do you have a relationship that isn't at its best? Do you want a particular "item" but know it really isn't in your budget? Do you struggle to keep your house as clean as you'd like?

It doesn't matter what type of battle we face. Each one is rooted in the spiritual realm, which makes it a *spiritual battle*. As you work through each week, keep in mind your current battle. When you develop your personal action plan, you'll be prepared to strategize with all that you learned. Take some time to journal about your current battle.

_____
_____
_____
_____
_____
_____
_____
_____
_____
_____

day 1

fighting in God's strength

Finally, be strong in the Lord and in his mighty power. (EPHESIANS 6:10)

"Be strong!" Do a Google search for "be strong memes" and hundreds of images come up. Page after page of "stay strong" quotes exist. But what does "Be strong" mean, anyway? We hear it when the chips are down. When we're struggling. Our friends want us to reach deep inside and find fortitude, or strength of character. It can mean saying *no* to things that aren't good for us. It can even mean saying *no* to good things that aren't in our best interests. Sometimes it means becoming physically strong–building strong muscles and increasing bone density.

Have you ever wanted to do something that you knew you weren't strong enough to do? But you wanted to do it badly enough, so you became strong enough? Or maybe you didn't really want to do it, but you knew you needed to, so you did whatever it took to make it happen.

Years ago, I ran a marathon. I was overweight and completely out of shape. Running a marathon was not something I ever thought I would do–or even consider doing. My idea of fun was reading a good book while curled up on the couch. Who would intentionally put her body through that? But God has a way of changing our perspective. That summer I read Henry Blackaby's book *Experiencing God* to prepare for teaching the same Bible study in the fall. I had just read this paragraph:

> God delights in using ordinary people to accomplish His divine purposes. Paul said God deliberately seeks out the weak and the despised things because it is from them that He receives the greatest glory (1 Corinthians 1:26-31). When God does exceptional things through unexceptional people, then others recognize that only God could have done it.

If you feel weak, limited, ordinary, you are the best material through which God can work![2]

The first thing I thought of was my weight. Ugh. I felt so out of shape that completing a marathon seemed beyond what I could accomplish. I quickly dismissed it. Certainly, God could use something else in my life. However, a friend of mine from Bible study had been talking to me about her marathon experience and how excited she was about her finishing time. She told me the Houston Marathon was approaching, and she would run that one, too. Then she had the gall to tell me I could take part–just by walking. Of course, I balked at her. Not two weeks later, another friend called to tell me about a training program for the Houston Marathon. And it had just started. She wanted me to jump in with her and go for it.

I was stunned. Surely this is not what God wanted to do in my life. It was definitely beyond my ability. If I completed it, a watching world would certainly say, "Only God!"

My husband told me to talk with an organizer and get information. (Wisdom from a multitude of counselors, right?) So I did. She explained the whole process–assuring me that if I followed the program, I would be successful. I called Tim back and shared my new information. He was completely supportive. I had a decision to make, and I didn't have a lot of time to make it, but I put the pieces together. I needed to get healthy. God showed me He wanted to do something extraordinary in my life. And the Holy Spirit prompted me with this opportunity. Then God provided a way to make it happen–extraordinarily.

I said *yes* to God. But I also knew I had to tell people. I couldn't start this quietly. I needed accountability before God and people for committing to something I knew was beyond my ability. I expected God to do the miraculous.

After six months of consistent training, I finished my marathon. The following year I ran a half-marathon. There is no way I could have woken up one day and run a marathon just because I thought it would be a fun thing to do. The preparation was long and hard. But I became strong enough (with God's help!) to do it.

GOD ALMIGHTY

God called Abraham to leave his family and move to a land He would later show him. He promised to make a great nation from him. Twenty-four years later, Abraham was 99 and Sarah was 89, both well past the age of bearing children, still waiting for God's promise. Once again, God promised Abraham he would become the father of nations. But this time, God told Him who He was.

When Abram was ninety-nine years old, the Lord appeared to him and said, "I am God Almighty; walk before me faithfully and be blameless. Then I will make my covenant between me and you and will greatly increase your numbers." (Genesis 17:1-2)

Later, Abraham told Isaac, his son of God's promise, "May God Almighty bless you and make you fruitful and increase your numbers until you become a community of peoples" (Genesis 28:3).

God confirmed the promise to Isaac's son Jacob, "And God said to him, 'I am God Almighty; be fruitful and increase in number. A nation and a community of nations will come from you, and kings will be among your descendants'" (Genesis 35:11). This is ***el shaddai***. God Almighty, who can keep every promise He makes.

el shaddai: GOD ALMIGHTY

Our enemy wages war against our spirits, our souls, and our physical lives. We must be strong in the Lord to have victory. There is no way we can fight him in our own strength, but we can with our ***el shaddai***. He strengthens us for the battle.

GOD'S POWER

In Ephesians 6:10, we see three "power" words: strong, mighty, and power. The table below shows each English word along with its corresponding Greek word and definition.[3]

English Word	Greek Word	Greek Meaning
Strong	*endunamoo*	To strengthen.
Mighty	*ischus*	To have physical strength. The ability to perform what one desires. Strength that has been demonstrated.
Power	*kratos*	The presence of prevailing power.

Our Part

The first power word is *strong*, or **endunamoo**, which means to strengthen. For any activity we want to excel in, we must build strength. If it's a physical activity, we build strong muscles that support that activity. For example, to run long distances, it's important to build strength and endurance. Strong glutes support your knees. Strong lungs and a strong core support your whole body so you can keep going when you're tired. If you want to excel in schoolwork so you have scholarship opportunities, it's important to do all your homework, to study well for tests, and to get tutoring for concepts difficult to understand.

It's the same for becoming strong in the Lord. We strengthen our relationship with Him through "spiritual disciplines" such as reading and studying the Bible, Scripture memory, prayer, service opportunities, and many other activities. We also develop spiritual strength by obeying God in the areas of our lives He puts His finger on, changing the ways we think and act so we align ourselves with His heart and His ways.

If you remember your grammar lessons, when a sentence starts with a verb, the implied subject is you. Paul is saying, "*You* be strong in the Lord." This is our part. It takes time and "practice." And Paul gave us a plan.

God's Part

The second power word is *mighty*, or **ischus**. It is the strength (or ability) that one has. It includes completeness, or maximizing personal potential.[4] In this case, it is God's strength–the strength we've seen Him demonstrate, or His proven strength. Reading through the Bible, we see repeatedly where God accomplished miracles. Nothing is too difficult for him (Jeremiah 32:27).

God's Power Demonstrated

The third power word is *power*, or **kratos**, which is prevailing power. Another way to express that is dominion. It's God's power over the world–creation, people, and His enemies.

In Genesis 1, God simply spoke. He said, "Let there be …" With His voice alone, He created light, life, and every rock, mountain, river, ocean, and animal.

> *Let them praise the name of the Lord, for at his command they were created.*
> (Psalm 148:5)

fighting in God's strength | day 1

By His word, God healed His people and rescued them (Psalm 107:19-20). Even now, every time He speaks, His word achieves every purpose for which He sends it (Isaiah 55:11).

When Jesus was in Capernaum, a Roman officer approached Him with a request. His servant was at home, suffering a terrible illness. Jesus offered to go with him, to heal the servant. But the Roman officer knew that Jesus was powerful. He said, "Just say the word, and my servant will be healed" (Matthew 8:9). Jesus told the officer, "Go! Let it be done just as you believed it would" (Matthew 8:13). With His voice alone, Jesus healed the man's servant.

A short time after that, Jesus and His disciples got into a boat to sail across the Sea of Galilee. Tired from ministry, Jesus took a nap. Meanwhile, a raging storm developed. Waves crashed over the boat, and it terrified the disciples. They woke up Jesus and begged Him to save them. Jesus commanded the winds and the waves, "Silence! Be still!" Immediately all was calm. If the disciples were afraid of the storm, they were even more terrified when they realized who was in the boat with them (Mark 4:41). I'm sure they recalled the psalmist's words.

He stilled the storm to a whisper; the waves of the sea were hushed. (Psalm 107:29)

In the Old Testament, we see God's powerful arm at work. God separated the Red Sea, and the Israelites crossed to safety on dry land! They didn't trudge through mud. God made the ground completely dry. Later, He fed them every day with bread and quail from heaven. In the middle of the desert, He provided water from a rock. God hurled large hailstones on the Amorites. Then He made the sun stand still so the Israelites could finish their battle and have victory. Through Elijah, God raised the dead to life. Through Elisha, He provided a miracle supply of oil for a poor widow. God allowed barren women to bear children.

In the New Testament, God chose a precious virgin girl to carry and give birth to His Son. The blind saw, the deaf heard, the mute spoke, and the lame walked. Many who died were raised to life. The greatest miracle of all was Jesus's resurrection from the dead. By His power, He rose to life, forever! Eventually, those of us who have accepted Christ's death on the cross as payment for our sin will also experience resurrection life by the same great power.

This is ***ischus kratos***. God's unlimited power demonstrated in the world. ***Ischus kratos*** is the power we have access to, but there is a difference in building and using your own strength and drawing strength from God's unlimited resources. Ephesians 1:18-22 is one prayer Paul prays for the church in Ephesus. He uses the same three power words here as he does in Ephesians 6:10.

> *I pray that the eyes of your heart may be enlightened in order that you may know the hope to which he has called you, the riches of his glorious inheritance in his holy people, and his incomparably great power for us who believe. That **power** is the same as the **mighty strength** he exerted when he raised Christ from the dead and seated him at his right hand in the heavenly realms.* (Ephesians 1:18-19, emphasis added)

The first occurrence of power in these verses is similar to the word *strength* in Ephesians 6:10. But there is a slight difference. The Greek word for power here is **dunamis** (or **dynamis**). Does it remind you of anything? It's where our word *dynamite* comes from.

Mighty strength is **ischus kratos**, God's unlimited power demonstrated in the world. Put together, it's something like this:

> I pray that… you may know… God's explosive power, which He gives us who believe. He demonstrated this unlimited power when He raised Christ from the dead.

No one, outside of God's power, has ever raised a body from the dead. Modern medicine can't do it. Incantations can't do it. It just doesn't happen. But we serve an all-powerful God, whose voice alone created everything from nothing. Much of the time my voice can't even move my own children into action. Lazarus was dead, dead, dead. But Jesus said, "Lazarus, come forth!" And he did! Paul wanted the Ephesians (and us) to experience this same power! In fact, he repeats this same message in many of his letters.

Reference	What	Why?
Ephesians 3:16	God would strengthen them with power through His Spirit in their inner being	So Christ would dwell in their hearts through faith
Ephesians 3:18	They would have the power to grasp how wide and long and high and deep is Christ's love	So they would know and be filled to all the fullness of God
Colossians 1:11	Strengthen them with all power according to His glorious might	So they would have great endurance and patience
2 Thessalonians 1:11	By his power	They could accomplish all the good things their faith prompted them to do.

But we also know that Paul was weak. God gave him some sort of weakness to keep him humble. Over and over, Paul asked God to remove it, but God did not. Instead, God told Paul that His grace was enough, that His power worked best in his weakness. Paul's resolve? To glory in his weakness so that Christ's power was on display (2 Corinthians 12:8-9).

In all his writings, Paul clarifies that only through God's mighty power was he able to preach the gospel (Colossians 1:29; Ephesians 1:7). He told the Philippians that he could do all things through Christ who strengthened him (Philippians 4:13).

APPROPRIATING POWER FOR EVERYDAY LIVING

First, we recognize that we have access to God's power and strength. We do not fight this battle on our own. If we tried, we would experience certain defeat. No matter what the memes say, Christians need God's power and strength to experience victory.

In the Old Testament, God promises to strengthen those who hope in Him. Even though we grow tired and weary, when we hope in God, He renews our strength and allows us to keep going (Isaiah 40:29-31). In the New Testament, Paul says, "For I can do everything through Christ, who gives me strength" (Philippians 4:13).

God's strength is available to us, but how do we get it? Remember when God told Paul that He would display His power in Paul's weakness? Let's look at that verse again.

> *Each time he said, "My grace is all you need. My power works best in weakness." So now I am glad to boast about my weaknesses, so that the power of Christ can work through me.* (2 Corinthians 12:9)

What is the first thing God told Paul? My grace is all you need. Whatever God calls you to, you can be sure He will enable you to do it. Often those things will be more than you can do in and of yourself. We still must do our part–which is taking the next step forward in obedience. As we do that, God meets us there and gives us strength for each subsequent step.

Grace follows obedience. The result is power.

POWER = OBEDIENCE + GRACE

Training for a marathon was unlike anything I had done before. I built and used my own strength as I trained. During the week we ran on our own, basing our workouts on time: twenty to twenty-five minutes to begin with. On the weekends we did our "long runs" with a group. I think the first Saturday was a 4-mile run. For a nonrunner, even this distance was overwhelming.

Each week was progressively more difficult. I remember praying, "God, I don't know how this will work." In my spirit, I felt the Lord say, "You do your part during the week, and I'll show up on the weekend." Not that He wasn't with me each day. He was. My part was to get dressed, lace up my shoes, and hit the treadmill. And keep going. He matched my effort beyond what I could do.

When Saturday came, I did the same thing. I got dressed, grabbed my fuel belt, and met with my group. We took off running, and God sustained me. Yes, I was exhausted when I got home. I remember crashing on the recliner with bags of ice on my knees. I often needed a nap later in the day.

The week before race day, the marathon committee changed the start time. The race officially started at 7:00 a.m. They allowed those who needed extra time to start at 6:30, but there was a catch. Those who started early would receive none of the swag for finishing. No medal, finishers T-shirt, mug, or other goodies.

Of course, I thought about it! But I sensed the Lord saying, "I called you to this. I will be with you. You need not start early. Yes, there will be pain! But you won't be alone." God was so sweet. I started with the 7:00 a.m. runners. I even had two friends jump in the race with me at key points to encourage me as I ran. Five hours, thirty-four minutes, and forty-eight seconds later, I crossed the finish line.

> God enables us to do everything He calls us to. As we move forward in obedience, God meets us there and gives us strength for each subsequent step.

I was faithful to train. I didn't train perfectly, to be sure. But every time I laced up, God met me on my treadmill or on the pavement. He provided encouragement from friends or just the right song on my playlist. Sometimes it was the joy of seeing the sun come up. I knew His presence in ways I had never experienced before.

I did my part. I trained. I strengthened my body, my mind, and my spirit. God did His part. He extended my ability. When I reached the end of my physical strength, He took my weakness and added His strength. Truly, a watching world said, "Only God!"

fighting in God's strength | day 1

When have you experienced God's strength when your strength ran out?

day 2

our enemy

For our struggle is not against flesh and blood, but against the rulers, against the authorities, against the powers of this dark world and against the spiritual forces of evil in the heavenly realms. (EPHESIANS 6:12)

If we expect to win any battle, we must have basic knowledge of our opponent. The more we know, the better our odds of winning. Matthew, Mark, and Luke record Jesus's encounter with Satan in the wilderness. Each account adds different details, which helps us see the big picture. For our own spiritual battles with Satan, let's see what we can learn about our enemy as he interacted with Jesus and His disciples.

JESUS'S TEMPTATION

At the beginning of Jesus's ministry, He went into the wilderness, where He fasted for forty days. Satan met Him there and tempted Him where He was most vulnerable. Yes, Jesus was God. But when He came to earth, He became a man and had the same physical and emotional needs that you and I have. The difference is, when Jesus faced temptation, He never yielded to it (Hebrews 4:15).

Read Luke 4:1-13.

Verse 2 tells us that not only did Jesus fast for 40 days, He was tempted by the devil during those 40 days. My guess is that Jesus was mentally weary, as well. We do not know the details of the 40 days of temptation. It may be that what we read at the "end of the 40 days" is the culmination of the same types of temptation He experienced the whole time. Satan tempted Jesus in three ways:

Physical Need

Jesus had been fasting for forty days and was hungry, plain and simple. The devil said, "If you are the Son of God, prove it! Turn this stone into bread!" Jesus was confident in who He was. The Bread of Life did not need to prove anything to Satan.

Purpose in Life

Satan knew that Jesus came to earth to defeat him. He offered an alternative strategy. Instead of the impending pain of death, Satan offered Jesus the world, if He would simply worship him. But Jesus knew that everything already belonged to God and was only on loan to the devil. Jesus loved you and me enough to say no to the easy way.

Power

As a last-ditch effort, Satan questioned Jesus's divinity with one more temptation: "If you are the Son of God, prove it by jumping off this cliff. I know the angels will rescue You!" At this point, Jesus had had enough and sent the devil on his way. Jesus was full of the Holy Spirit and did not give in to the temptation. Verse 13 says Satan left Jesus until the next opportunity came. Satan never gives up!

1. **For each temptation, Satan began with an "if" question. When has Satan tempted you by questioning with an "if"?**

   _____
   _____
   _____
   _____

2. **Read John 8:44 and John 10:10. Note how Jesus describes the devil.**

   _____
   _____
   _____
   _____

3. Read 1 Peter 5:8 and 2 Corinthians 4:4. Note what else we learn about our enemy.

___

4. Write out James 4:7 and emphasize what happens when we resist the devil!

___

Satan is a liar and a deceiver whose goal is to destroy believers. He will use any means possible to do so. But when we remain alert and resist Him, he will flee!

THE BATTLE

Although we do not see the actual spiritual battle, we see the results in our world and in people.

5. Read Ephesians 1:18-21 below and underline any power words you find.

> *I pray that the eyes of your heart may be enlightened in order that you may know ... his incomparably great power for us who believe. That power is the same as the mighty strength he exerted when he raised Christ from the dead and seated him at his right hand in the heavenly realms, far above all rule and authority, power and dominion, and every name that is invoked, not only in the present age but also in the one to come.*
> (Ephesians 1:18–21)

6. Ephesians 6:12 describes the powers of darkness. How do they contrast with what you underlined above?

___

week 1 | standing firm in Christ

7. Read Romans 8:37-39. Do we have any reason to fear? Why or why not?

_____

_____

_____

Yes, unseen powers are at work in our world. But God is bigger! God is stronger! Nothing can ever separate us from Him or His love for us. When we find ourselves amid difficult days, fearful and worried, we can know with confidence that no power of hell or scheme of the devil can keep us from our God who loves us.

Although the battle is fierce and our enemy clever and determined, we need not be afraid. We have God's limitless power at our disposal, a panoply of armor to protect us, and the most effective weapons for defeating our enemy.

> *Going Deeper:* This is our first BibleGateway search. Go to www.biblegateway.com. (For detailed instructions, refer to the Appendix on page 199.
> In the search bar at the top, type the word power, *and press enter. Then, filter your results by selecting the book of Ephesians on the far right. Do the same thing for the words* might *and* strength. *Note the number of times these words are used. Power is a strong theme in the Book of Ephesians.*

day 3

take your stand

Put on the full armor of God, so that you can take your stand against the devil's schemes. For our struggle is not against flesh and blood, but against the rulers, against the authorities, against the powers of this dark world and against the spiritual forces of evil in the heavenly realms. Therefore put on the full armor of God, so that when the day of evil comes, you may be able to stand your ground, and after you have done everything, to stand. Stand firm then, with the belt of truth buckled around your waist, with the breastplate of righteousness in place. (EPHESIANS 6:11-14)

Today is important in our study, as it forms the foundation for applying the lessons we learn from this point forward. Paul tells us how we are to respond to opposing spiritual forces. Paul instructed Timothy to "flee the evil desires of youth." In other words, he told Timothy not to feed his passions. Instead, Timothy was to pursue the godly characteristics of righteousness, faith, love, and peace–which flow from a pure heart (2 Timothy 2:22). We may have to remove ourselves from certain situations, but we still battle the enemy.

In the verses above, underline or highlight the phrases where you find the word *stand*. Each one of these phrases means something a little different, but an expository dictionary helps us understand them better.

The following chart will help us understand what each of them means and how they are used in this passage.[5]

week 1 | standing firm in Christ

Word or Phrase	Greek	Definition
Take your stand against the devil's schemes (v. 11)	*hístēmi*	Instead of running away, stand.
Stand your ground (v. 13a)	*anthístēmi*	Go stand against, resist in deed or word.
Stand (v. 13b)	*hístēmi*	Instead of running away, stand.
Stand firm, then (v. 14)	*hístēmi*	Instead of running away, stand.

Hístēmi means to stand in the face of evil. When we face evil, our first impulse may be to run away. We may even feel like melting into the ground. But that is not what Paul says we are to do. We are to stand in the face of our enemy, but we don't just stand.

Anthístēmi is a little different. "Stand your ground" carries the idea of resisting! We actively, in word and in deed, oppose our enemy. Yes, it is a scary thing! But we have the power of God in us and on our side. We can stand firm against our enemy and experience victory!

1. **Skim Exodus 14 and then stop at verse 13. What did God tell Moses and the Israelites to do, and what would be the result?**

   _____
   _____
   _____
   _____

2. **Write out 1 John 4:4, and emphasize who is in us and how this affects our spiritual battles.**

   _____
   _____
   _____
   _____

God is in the business of fighting for His people. He did it in the Old Testament. He did it in the New Testament. And He will do it for you!

3. According to 2 Thessalonians 2:15, what is one way we stand firm?

_____

_____

_____

4. Summarize what it means to stand your ground.

_____

_____

_____

We aren't perfect; we *will* fall. When we do, Satan will heap guilt on us. He would have us believe we are failures, unworthy of God's love, and unable to stand again; but those are lies. God forgives us and gives us second chances—over and over again (Lamentations 3:22-23). God enters our messes, lift us out of us out of them, and sets our feet on a broad plane where we can stand firm once again (Psalm 31:8; Psalm 40:2).

Satan does NOT want us to stand firm, and he'll do anything he can to make us doubt what God says.

5. Read the passage below and underline what happens when we doubt.

> *If any of you lacks wisdom, you should ask God, who gives generously to all without finding fault, and it will be given to you. But when you ask, you must believe and not doubt, because the one who doubts is like a wave of the sea, blown and tossed by the wind. That person should not expect to receive anything from the Lord. Such a person is double-minded and unstable in all they do.* (James 1:5–8)

week 1 | standing firm in Christ

6. When have you had to stand your ground and not doubt?

_____
_____
_____
_____

We are to stand firm. But how do we do that? Each week, after we've studied each piece of the armor, we will evaluate how our enemy attacks us, how God's armor protects us from those attacks, and what we can do to stand firm.

> *Now it is God who makes both us and you stand firm in Christ. He anointed us, set his seal of ownership on us, and put his Spirit in our hearts as a deposit, guaranteeing what is to come ... It is by faith you stand firm.* (2 Corinthians 1:21-24)

> ***Going Deeper:*** *Do a BibleGateway search for* stand firm *or* standing firm *and see what you find.*

day 4

in Christ

Remain in me, as I also remain in you. No branch can bear fruit by itself; it must remain in the vine. Neither can you bear fruit unless you remain in me. (JOHN 15:4)

As mentioned earlier, putting on the armor of God is not so much about how we pray but about how we live. Our prayer life affects how we live, and how we live affects how we pray. Standing firm against our enemy is different. It's about our life in Christ. The key is the two-letter word *in*. It's about staying connected to our Source of life.

When my kids were small, a neighbor friend of their grandparents sent them home with a jar containing some leaves. Hidden inside was a pupa, or chrysalis. Every day they watched it grow until the butterfly inside made its way outside. They were thrilled! So was I! So much so that I planted a passion vine, thinking that would attract caterpillars. And it did! We got to see several butterflies go through metamorphosis.

Except, that vine!

What was once a source of pleasure became an annoyance. The main vine had the passionflower blooms, but that's not all there is to a vine. They have little tendrils that grow (quite quickly) and wrap around anything within reach. They help support the vine, but they also choke other plants if you don't stay on top of them. They can become invasive if you don't prune them regularly. I learned that, although I enjoyed the flowers and the butterflies, I was not a vinedresser.

Vinedressers cultivate and prune their vines. They care about the vine and its fruit. For grapevines, their goal is to grow quality grapes that will be used for making wine, grape juice, or raisins. Many of those grapes find their way into our homes for snacking.

week 1 | standing firm in Christ

Cultivating includes planting, watering, feeding, and pulling weeds when necessary. Pruning is cutting away dead wood or anything that takes away life from the main trunk. A pruned vine yields more fruit.

1. **Read John 15:1-11.**

What does the relationship between the vine and the vinedresser/gardener represent?

_____
_____

What does the relationship between the vine and the branch represent?

_____
_____

What does the relationship between the vinedresser/gardener and the branch represent?

_____
_____

What does it mean to abide in Christ?

_____
_____
_____

2. **According to John 15:4-5, 8, 11, what is evident in our lives as we abide in Christ?**

_____
_____
_____

3. Is this evident in your life?

_____
_____
_____
_____

Jesus told His disciples that they could not bear fruit if they were not connected to Him, the True Vine. Then He made this profound statement:

Apart from me, you can do nothing. (John 15:5b)

If we do not abide in Christ, we will not bear fruit. Neither will we be successful at any of our endeavors–including putting on the armor of God and standing firm against our enemy. Abiding in Christ is essential.

day 5

When we abide in Christ, His life and power flow through our "spiritual veins," enabling us to battle our enemy effectively.

personal action plan

Where do you feel weak in your spiritual battle?

_____
_____
_____
_____
_____
_____
_____
_____
_____

What Scriptures help you stand firm in God's strength?

_____
_____
_____
_____
_____
_____
_____
_____

week 1 | standing firm in Christ

___

Using the verses you chose, write a battlefield prayer expressing your desire to live firmly connected to your Source of life.

___

What songs reminds you that God fights for you?
What songs helps you stay connected to your Source of life?

___

week two – the sword of the Spirit

day 1 – the Word of God

day 2 – the sword of the Spirit

day 3 – the enemy of the Word of God

day 4 – standing firm with the sword of the Spirit

day 5 – personal action plan

week 2 | standing firm in Christ

weekly prep

What is your current battle? Last week's struggle may have been resolved, or your situation may have become more dire. This week you may have a new issue. Whatever the case, let's take it to the Lord as we prepare to learn how to use God's Word, the Sword of the Spirit, as a weapon to fight our spiritual battles.

_____
_____
_____
_____
_____
_____
_____
_____
_____
_____
_____
_____
_____
_____
_____
_____
_____
_____

day 1

the Word of God

For you have been born again, not of perishable seed, but of imperishable, through the living and enduring word of God. (1 PETER 1:23)

We will use the following words and phrases interchangeably: *God's Word, the Word of God, the Bible, and Scripture.*

Before we approach the Word of God, we must decide if we will believe the words we read. Skeptics approach with doubt, but we can approach God's Word with confidence.

And the words of the Lord are flawless, like silver purified in a crucible, like gold refined seven times. (Psalm 12:6)

Your promises have been thoroughly tested, and your servant loves them. (Psalm 119:140)

I love the phrase "thoroughly tested." Other translations say "pure," which makes sense when you think about how gold is purified through fire. The psalmist has personal experience with God's Word meeting him at his point of need–through the fire of suffering.

WHAT IS THE WORD OF GOD?

When we study the Bible, it's important to lay a foundation of faith. First, we decide if we believe God is who He says He is. Then we decide if we will believe the Bible, His written word to us. When we affirm these two things, we accept the responsibility for responding to what we read.

Typically, the phrase *Word of God* refers to God's written Word, the Bible. In the church world, this phrase is used all the time. Because of that, it's easy to become numb to what it really is. Let's not do that. Let's remember that any time we read the Bible, we hear God, the Creator of the universe, speak. Every written word is God's message to us as a community and individually.

> *All Scripture is God-breathed.* (2 Timothy 3:16a)

> *Above all, you must understand that no prophecy of Scripture came about by the prophet's own interpretation of things. For prophecy never had its origin in the human will, but prophets, though human, spoke from God as they were carried along by the Holy Spirit.* (2 Peter 1:20-21)

These are the defining passages for the veracity of the Bible. Although the Bible was penned by humans, God inspired Scripture. And because He did, we can trust that He made sure every word written (within the personality of the writers) was exactly as He wanted. It is accurate and trustworthy.

WHAT ARE THE PURPOSES OF GOD'S WORD?

God's Word accomplishes everything that He intends for it to (Isaiah 55:10-11). God has a purpose every time we hear or read God's Word. His primary purpose is to lead us to an eternal relationship with Him, which begins with salvation.

> *But these are written that you may believe that Jesus is the Messiah, the Son of God, and that by believing you may have life in his name.* (John 20:31)

Salvation

The overarching story of the Bible is God's love for mankind and His plan for our redemption. From the beginning, God created us to have fellowship with Him. But sin ruined that relationship and separated us from God. Because God loves us so much, He made a way for fellowship with Him to be restored. The penalty for sin is death, and He gave us His Son to pay that penalty (Romans 6:23). Jesus exchanged places with us and died a criminal's death. Then He rose from the grave, demonstrating His power over the grave!

When we confess our sin and accept His death in place of ours, our relationship with God is restored. He cleanses us from our sin. From that point forward, everything changes. We are new creations in Christ (2 Corinthians 5:17), and our lives reflect His character. Instead of spending eternity separated from God, we will live in heaven with Him forever. If you've never encountered Jesus, you can read more in the Appendix on page 208.

Continual Cleansing

The Bible is alive and rich with truth. Unlike with any other book, we can read a verse or passage repeatedly and gain new insight each time. Sometimes, God's Word reveals things we don't want to see. The Holy Spirit works on our inner person, helping us to understand our true thoughts and attitudes, which sometimes are hard for us to discern (Hebrews 4:12).

> *Husbands, love your wives, just as Christ loved the church and gave himself up for her to make her holy, cleansing her by the washing with water through the word, and to present her to himself as a radiant church, without stain or wrinkle or any other blemish, but holy and blameless.* (Ephesians 5:25-27)

God's desire is for us to be conformed to the image of His Son (Romans 8:29). Transformation doesn't happen overnight. It's a lifelong process. God gently guides us as we spend time reading His Word. As we yield our wills to His, we move toward becoming the person God wants us to be (2 Corinthians 3:18). This is the cleansing process of God's Word.

As parents, we discipline our children. When our kids move into the teenage years, they often resist correction. Because we love them, we keep at it. We know what's ahead. We know the pitfalls they will fall into if they don't listen and learn. Our goal is for them to become responsible, independent adults. We want them to live in freedom. It's the same with God's Word. The apostle James tells us:

> *But whoever looks intently into the perfect law that gives freedom, and continues in it–not forgetting what they have heard, but doing it–they will be blessed in what they do.*
> (James 1:25)

God blesses our obedience when we do what He says. He doesn't want us trapped by sin and all the entanglements that go with it. God's Word cleanses us so we can be free!

ENCOURAGEMENT

In the regular course of our Bible reading, God provides the right Scripture to strengthen our souls. Over time, we collect treasured verses we return to for the encouragement we need.

God's Word Gives Us Hope

Hope is a beautiful word. It is pregnant with the expectation of good things to come! Hope keeps us moving forward. Biblical hope tells us that God keeps all His promises. We need this hope every day–not only when we are feeling hopeless.

You are my refuge and my shield; your word is my source of hope. (Psalm 119:14)

For everything that was written in the past was written to teach us, so that through the endurance taught in the Scriptures and the encouragement they provide we might have hope. (Romans 15:4)

Spending time in God's Word every day anchors our hearts in His faithfulness. Hope in God's Word is not a maybe hope, like I hope my package arrives before Wednesday. Biblical hope is secure and trustworthy because it is based on God's character.

God's Word Brings Us Joy

Quality time with my grown kids is hard to come by. All are busy with work, college courses, or outings with friends. When an opportunity to visit with any of them presents itself, I drop everything, even if I am simply a distraction from their homework.

By entering their world, I get to know them better. As they mature and seek independence, parts of their lives are a bit mysterious. They don't share everything with me like they used to. Time with these "children" of mine brings joy to my heart. I experience delight when I'm with them, and I learn new aspects of their personalities or their character.

Like with any other relationship, spending quality time with God is how we get to know Him. As we read, study, and pray, we begin to recognize His voice when He speaks to us, collecting favorite verses along the way. We can say, as the psalmists did:

The precepts of the Lord are right, giving joy to the heart. (Psalm 19:8a)

Your statutes are my heritage forever; they are the joy of my heart. (Psalm 119:111)

GUIDANCE

God's Word is an instruction manual for life. It contains everything we need for successful living. No other book is as powerful and practical as the Bible. From simple, everyday choices (whom the Word of God | day 1

to hang out with and how we spend our money) to the big things in our lives (whom to marry and where we should live), God's Word can guide every decision we make.

> *All Scripture is God-breathed and is useful for teaching, rebuking, correcting and training in righteousness, so that the servant of God may be thoroughly equipped for every good work.* (2 Timothy 3:16-17)

God's Word teaches what is true and right, shows us where we are wrong and how to correct it, and prepares and equips us for all God calls us to. Proverbs is probably the most practical book in the Bible. My dad taught me to love this book. Since it has 31 chapters and most months have 31 days, you can read a chapter a day as part of your quiet time. The introduction to the Book of Proverbs states that its purpose is to teach all kinds of people how to gain wisdom and understanding (Proverbs 1:2-4), including the simple-minded person (Proverbs 19:7b). God's Word guides and

> Let's not become numb to what the Word of God really is. Any time we read the Bible, we hear God, the Creator of the universe, speak.

transforms our thinking (Romans 12:2). No longer do we have to make poor choices. We can now make wise choices! The key to successful decision-making? Spending time in God's Word every day.

> *Your word is a lamp for my feet a light on my path.* (Psalm 119:105)

> *Commit to the Lord whatever you do, and he will establish your plans.* (Proverbs 16:3)

The Hebrew word for *plans* in Proverbs 16:3 means thoughts. God causes our thoughts to become aligned with His thoughts. What choices are facing you today? Are you evaluating relationships, investments, medical issues? Are you considering a ministry direction? Whatever it is, you can trust God's Word to guide you each step of the way.

RECEIVING THE WORD OF GOD

Texas droughts cause the ground to be dry and hard, but regular rain makes it soft and moist. I'm amazed at how fast grass grows after a good rain. You can cut it short one Saturday morning, and if it rains for a few days afterward, it will be a jungle by the following Saturday. If I want to put in new plants, I'm grateful for the moist soil. It's much easier to dig up the dirt to make a home for a new plant.

Jesus explained to His disciples that the soil of our hearts determines how we grow in response to His Word. He explained that when a sower scatters seed in his fields, some seeds land on the road, some land in rocks or thorns, and others in good, moist soil. Those that land in good soil take root and produce a large crop (Luke 8:1-8).

The soil represents our hearts. The Holy Spirit is like the rain. If our hearts are hard, we won't respond well to what the Holy Spirit shows us in God's Word. But if our hearts are tender, then we will respond and be effective for Christ.

WE MEET GOD ON THE PAGES OF SCRIPTURE

How we approach God's Word is as important as our time in it. If we hurry, we may not hear God speak clearly. Our hearts will be like the fallow ground that doesn't receive the seed well. Slowing down doesn't mean we have to read for a long time. It does mean we still ourselves long enough to hear God speak. It may mean reading something more than once, thinking carefully about it so we can see how God wants to use it in our lives.

Knowing we are entering God's presence should have a profound impact on our time with Him. He is always present everywhere, but God meets us in a special way on the pages of Scripture. It's where He speaks the most clearly. God's Word is where we receive the vital nutrients we need to grow in our Christian walk. It's where we get to know God's heart as Father. It's how we know He truly loves us. It is the foundation of our life with Him.

> *Let the morning bring me word of your unfailing love, for I have put my trust in you. Show me the way I should go, for to you I entrust my life. (Psalms 143:8)*

> ***Going Deeper:*** *Do a BibleGateway search for "word of God" in quotation marks. Also search for "word of the Lord." Note how many times you find this phrase in your Bible. (This doesn't include "voice of God," "God spoke," "God said," or other indicators of God speaking.) Skim through the results. What do you notice about the context of each verse? What is "the word of God" in reference to? Who is speaking?*

the Word of God | day 1

What keeps you too busy to hear God speak?

_____
_____
_____
_____
_____
_____
_____
_____
_____
_____

What intentional, practical ways can you slow down so you can hear God speak?

_____
_____
_____
_____
_____
_____
_____
_____
_____
_____
_____
_____
_____
_____

day 2

the sword of the Spirit

Take the helmet of salvation and the sword of the Spirit, which is the word of God.
(EPHESIANS 6:17)

In a heated argument intending to make a point, has anyone ever said to you, "Those were your exact words!" I have been told that. I have even said that. The words that come tumbling out of our mouths stick with people, especially if they are said during an emotional moment. Good or bad, intentionally or unintentionally, our words count. They will either hurt or they will heal (Proverbs 18:21). Consider for a moment, why Paul called this weapon the Sword of the Spirit. It's interesting that the word *sword* contains the word, *word*. Yes, it is a nuance of the English language, but interesting, nonetheless.

THE POWER OF WORDS

1. Read the following verses from Proverbs and describe the power of our spoken words.

Proverbs 12:18, 25; 15:1, 4; 16:24; 25:18

_____
_____
_____
_____
_____

#standingfirmbiblestudy

2. Read the following verses and describe how God's Word gives life.

John 1:1-4; 6:63, 68; Philippians 2:14-16

_____

_____

_____

_____

_____

God's Word has the power to give life! First it shows us our need for a Savior. When we give our lives to Christ, we receive eternal life! But God's Word is a gift for every day, as well.

> *Going Deeper: Do a BibleGateway search with the words* word *and* life, *not in quotation marks, to discover other verses that discuss how God's Word gives life. Note the suggested result at the top of the list. How does this expand your understanding of God's Word?*

During the Vietnam War, many Christian soldiers were taken prisoner. Their conditions were horrible. But somehow these Christian soldiers found one another. They developed a code they used to encourage each other with Scriptures they had memorized. Sometimes one prisoner would remember part, and another prisoner would remember the rest. Although they were in solitary confinement, they developed a way to worship as a community. Eventually, to make room for more prisoners, many were imprisoned in larger cells. For years they asked for a Bible. Finally, they were given one. They read passages and memorized 1 Corinthians 13 in the two short hours they had it. Later they could have a Bible for one hour a week. They copied as much as they could during that time. The life-giving Word of God sustained them through their tortuous imprisonment.[6]

We can be encouraged simply by reading our Bibles. We can easily encourage others by sharing Scriptures with them via texts, phone calls, cards, and emails.

3. Whom do you know who has survived suffering by clinging to the Word of God?

_____
_____
_____

4. Whom do you know who needs encouragement from the life-giving Word of God?

_____
_____
_____

THE HOLY SPIRIT AND GOD'S WORD

The Holy Spirit has special roles in the believer's life. He convicts us of sin and convinces us of our need for a Savior (John 16:8). Our "new birth" results from regeneration by the Spirit (John 3:5-8). The Holy Spirit indwells and seals all believers (1 Corinthians 3:16; 2 Corinthians 1:20-22). As our faith grows, we display the fruit (or character) of the Holy Spirit (Galatians 5:22-23). And that's not all!

5. Read the following verses, and underline what else the Holy Spirit does for us.

> *But the Advocate, the Holy Spirit, whom the Father will send in my name, will teach you all things and will remind you of everything I have said to you.* (John 14:26)

> *But when he, the Spirit of truth, comes, he will guide you into all the truth. He will not speak on his own; he will speak only what he hears, and he will tell you what is yet to come.* (John 16:13)

God's Word is not just any sword. It is the Holy Spirit's sword. He wrote it for us and helps us understand it. Because we have studied it well, He can bring to mind exactly what we need when we are in the heat of battle.

day 3

the enemy of the Word of God

The tempter came to him and said, "If you are the Son of God, tell these stones to become bread." (MATTHEW 4:3)

The Sword of the Spirit is our primary weapon against Satan. In fact, our other weapons, prayer and praise, are based on the Word of God. The Word of God is powerful! It reveals the heart of the Father toward us, leading us to salvation. It guides our lives and protects us from the enemy of our souls. It's no wonder Satan wants to keep us from it.

1. **Consider your quiet time with God. What gets in the way of your reading your Bible?**

_____
_____
_____
_____
_____
_____

This isn't a judgment question. It's just to get you thinking. All of us, at one time or another, set aside God's Word. What's interesting, though, is that when we miss a few days of reading, it's easy to miss a few weeks, or months. When we don't read our Bibles, we don't have what we need to stand firm against our enemy. Our swords become dull and unwieldy.

Satan knows mankind well, and he knows us individually. He knows when and where we're vulnerable. He will exploit that. Yes, he is fearsome. But the One who is in us is greater than the one who wants to destroy us (1 John 4:4).

2. **Read Genesis 3:1. What question did the serpent ask Eve?**

_____

Last week we reviewed how Satan tempted Jesus in Luke's gospel. This week, we will look at it in the Gospel of Matthew.

3. **Read Matthew 4:1-11. How did Satan tempt Jesus?**

_____
_____
_____
_____

Satan knows Scripture well. He knows what God expects and distorts God's Word to cause us to question what God said. Sometimes he out and out lies about what God said. Therefore, it's important to discern truth from error.

In this passage, Jesus was physically weak. Since He was human and experienced temptation in every way, just like you and me (Hebrews 4:15), I think it's safe to say that He was emotionally and mentally weak, as well. This is just where Satan wanted Him. He attacked Jesus where He was vulnerable. First, Satan appealed to His physical needs by challenging Him to turn stones into bread. Then Satan challenged Him to prove His identity by jumping off a cliff, so His Father would send angels to rescue Him. Finally, Satan challenged Christ's purpose by offering an easier way to gain the worship of the world. He does the same to you and me. He knows when and where we are most vulnerable, and he attacks us there.

4. When are you most vulnerable to temptation?

_____
_____
_____
_____

Satan will also try to convince us that we cannot understand God's Word or that it's too hard to do what God wants us to do. So we give up in defeat.

5. Read 1 Corinthians 10:13. Recall what we learned about the Holy Spirit from Day 2. What is one way the Holy Spirit helps us escape temptation?

_____
_____
_____

The enemy wants to keep us from our Bibles. He will tempt us to sleep in or distract us with social media. He'll do anything. A family crisis may interrupt our quiet time or the work God calls us to. Even our loved ones are not off-limits.

He knows that God's Word is what stops him in his tracks, so he does whatever he can to keep us from it!

6. When have you been derailed from your daily time with God?

_____
_____
_____
_____

day 4

standing firm with the sword of the Spirit

Take the helmet of salvation and the sword of the Spirit, which is the word of God.
(EPHESIANS 6:17)

When was the last time you heard a song on the radio that you fell in love with? You downloaded it from your favorite platform and played it over and over until you knew it by heart. What happens when you do that? The song sticks with you. It's almost like background music to your day. No one else hears it, but you hear the melody and the words running through your mind. The song takes root in your heart.

Perhaps you have a letter containing the last written words of someone you loved. The words are written not only on paper but also on your heart. You've read them over and over, and you'll never forget them.

This is what happens when you take in something you love. It takes root in your heart. The words are always with you, surfacing with the slightest hint of something related to them.

In much the same way, God wants His words to take root in our hearts so we never forget them. The Sword of the Spirit, God's Word, is our primary weapon against Satan. Like an excellent soldier, we must learn to wield it well.

When Nehemiah returned to Jerusalem to rebuild the city walls, he posted armed officers near the workers to protect them from their enemies. The officers, however, weren't the only ones who carried weapons. The workers themselves kept their own swords at their sides so they would be ready to use them if necessary (Nehemiah 4:16-23). Like these workers, we need to have Scripture ready at a moment's notice.

The Greek language has several words we translate as *word* in English. Probably the one people think of most often is *logos*. Typically, it is used to describe Jesus, as the "word made flesh" (John 1:1), or the Bible as the written Word, as in the parable of the sower (Luke 8). In Ephesians 6:17, the Greek word is **rhema**. There are two parts that make it powerful. Let's look at Jesus's example and see if we can discover them.

JESUS IS OUR EXAMPLE

After His baptism and prior to the beginning of His public ministry, Jesus went into the desert for 40 days to fast and pray. At the end of that time, Satan came and tempted Him. Remember, although Jesus was fully God, He was also fully human–just like you and me–and faced every kind of temptation that we have (Hebrews 4:15). After 40 days of fasting, He was hungry and vulnerable.

1. **Read Matthew 4:1-11 again. Identify how Jesus responded to temptation.**

_____

_____

Jesus was physically weak, but He was strong in His Spirit. With each temptation, Jesus did two things. Did you see them? First, Jesus countered Satan's attack (lies) with the truth of God's Word–Scripture appropriate for the situation. Second, He spoke that Scripture–out loud. That's what **rhema** is–the spoken word.[7]

When I think of **rhema**, I think how **logos** becomes **rhema** when the right Scripture for the right moment is spoken aloud. For **rhema** to be effective, however, we must be thoroughly acquainted with passages that speak to our specific needs. When our enemy tempts us, we can do what Jesus did. We recall Scriptures specific to our situation and speak them aloud. We stand firm in the truth of God's Word. As we do that, God strengthens us against temptation.

There are many ways to deepen our understanding of Scripture. Memorization is one way. I can hear you now: "I can't memorize! I've tried and tried, and I just can't do it!" Dear friend, I say this because I care about you and want God's best for you. That right there is a lie from your enemy. The truth is: You can memorize God's Word. It is possible–for you!

2. **Read Psalm 119:9, 11. What are the benefits of memorizing God's Word?**

_____

_____

_____

If God used David to emphasize the importance of hiding God's Word in our hearts, then He knows we can do it, too. The Holy Spirit living in us will strengthen us to do so.

For many people, repetition is effective for memorizing Scripture. Repetition is good! In fact, God told the Israelites to write His Word everywhere and talk about it all the time (Deuteronomy 6:8-9). But memorization is not the only way to increase our understanding. In-depth study also helps Scripture take root in your heart, sometimes more effectively. When you meditate on God's Word, examine it inside and out, and apply its principles to your life, it becomes a part of you. You may not have every pronoun memorized, but you will know the Scriptures you studied.

3. **Read Psalm 1:1-3. What results from meditating on God's Word?**

_____

_____

_____

_____

4. **Read Colossians 3:16 below in the Amplified version. What does it mean to let the Word of God dwell richly among you?**

> *Let the word [spoken by] Christ (the Messiah) have its home [in your hearts and minds] and dwell in you in [all its] richness, as you teach and admonish and train one another in all insight and intelligence and wisdom [in spiritual things, and as you sing] psalms and hymns and spiritual songs, making melody to God with [His] grace in your hearts.*
> (Colossians 3:16, AMP)

_____

_____

_____

When we take time to study and memorize God's Word, it settles deep in our souls and transforms us. Because we desire to be like Christ, certain sins don't appeal to us anymore; but Satan doesn't give up. He tries to wear us down with the onslaught of overwhelming circumstances. He continues to tempt us in areas where we are vulnerable. He wants us to doubt God's love and power.

This is battle and battle is never easy. In these moments of need, the Holy Spirit brings to the surface the Word of God that has been stored in our hearts. As we stand firm on God's Word, repeating it out loud if necessary, the Sword of the Spirit becomes our weapon to overcome sin. God strengthens us against temptation and gives us the ability to endure.

> *Going Deeper*: *I developed an exercise to teach you how to study just one verse so through the process God's Word takes root in your heart. You can find it in the Appendix on page 202.*

day 5

The Word of God is our primary weapon in fighting our enemy. In order to use it well, we must know it well.

personal action plan

In what ways do you struggle to store God's Word in your heart?

_____
_____
_____
_____
_____
_____
_____
_____

What Scriptures remind you of the power of God's Word to defeat your enemy?

_____
_____
_____
_____
_____
_____
_____
_____

week 2 | standing firm in Christ

Write a battlefield prayer expressing your desire to wield God's Word well.

Find three songs that echo the power of God's Word.

week three – powerful prayer

day 1 – prayer that makes a difference

day 2 – how we pray

day 3 – the enemy of prayer

day 4 – standing firm in prayer

day 5 – personal action plan

week 3 | standing firm in Christ

weekly prep

This week we learn the key role prayer plays in our spiritual battles. Effective prayer takes effort and focus. When these are lacking, praying can be its own spiritual battle! Take some time to journal your thoughts about your prayer life.

_____
_____
_____
_____
_____
_____
_____
_____
_____
_____
_____
_____
_____
_____
_____
_____
_____

day 1

prayer that makes a difference

Then you will call on me and come and pray to me, and I will listen to you.
(JEREMIAH 29:12)

Prayer is simply communicating with God. It's a conversation. We speak—God listens. God speaks—we listen. For many people, prayer is a list of requests they take to God, hoping He'll say yes. For others it's the ongoing conversation in their heads. Still others spend hours on their knees. Each is part of prayer and has its place in our prayer life.

Prayer is much more than either of these. While God wants us to bring all our needs to Him (1 Peter 5:7), we must remember that prayer is also a conversation with the Creator of the universe. Prayer is the gateway to God's presence. God is all-powerful. When we enter His presence, we encounter His power to change the world and our lives. God planned for prayer to be a mechanism for accomplishing His purposes. When we pray, we become a part of what moves His hand.

PRAYER IN ACTION

The first half of the Book of Exodus details Israel's departure from Egypt. God protected them from the plagues He rained down on Egypt. When Moses led them out of slavery, God moved the Egyptians to give them various gold and silver articles and clothing for their journey. Shortly thereafter, Pharaoh changed his mind and pursued the Israelites to enslave them again, but God protected them. The Israelites crossed the Red Sea on dry land and escaped Pharaoh's army, which drowned while in hot pursuit. In the wilderness, God provided water from a rock when the Israelites were thirsty, manna every day, and quail when they craved meat. He gave them victory over the Amalekites, their first encounter with an opposing nation.

God proved Himself faithful and loving. He supplied everything they needed. Food, water, clothing, protection from warring nations, even the gold and silver that would later be used in the Tabernacle. God provided all of it for them. When they arrived at Mount Sinai, all of Israel gathered together. Moses consecrated them to the Lord, and they agreed to do everything God told them to do. Moses went to the top of the mountain to receive the Ten Commandments. God met him there in a cloud of dense smoke and displayed His awesome power with thunder and lightning. There God gave him the Ten Commandments. To top it off, a heavenly being blasted a trumpet like the Israelites had never heard. They were terrified! But Moses told them not to be afraid. God was testing them so they would reverence Him appropriately and not sin. Then God told Moses to tell them:

> *You have seen for yourselves that I have spoken to you from heaven: Do not make any gods to be alongside me; do not make for yourselves gods of silver or gods of gold.*
> (Exodus 20:22-23)

Moses stayed on the mountain for 40 days while God gave him the laws Israel would live by. When he came down the mountain, he heard the Israelites celebrating. To his dismay, they weren't worshiping God. Instead, they had made a golden calf and were worshiping it. After all God had done for them, they worshiped the created rather than their Creator. God was so angry that He told Moses to leave Him alone so He could destroy them. He would start over and make His covenant with Moses instead of Israel.

> Prayer is the gateway to God's presence. God is all-powerful. When we enter His presence, we encounter His power to change the world and our lives.

And this is the key. Moses stood between God and Israel and prayed on their behalf. He begged God not to destroy them but to forgive them. Because of Moses's plea, God relented from His anger and did not destroy them.

> *Therefore, He said He would destroy them. [And He would have done so] had not Moses, His chosen one, stepped into the breach before Him to turn away His threatening wrath.*
> (Psalm 106:23 AMP)

God used Moses's prayers as a way of accomplishing His purposes for Israel. I don't think prayer "changes God's mind" so much as it moves His hand, so to speak. God stirs our hearts to pray for what stirs His heart. As we pray, He accomplishes His purposes, and we get to play a role. It's a great privilege to be used by God in this way.

WHAT MAKES PRAYER POWERFUL?

James describes the prayers of a righteous person as effective and *powerful*–prayer that produces results (James 5:16). If you're remembering our power words from our first day (see page 5), then you're on the right path!

This is **ischus**, the ability to do what one desires. Strength that has been demonstrated. In this verse, however, **ischus** is combined with another word that means "much," so we're talking about *significant* power here. James said the prayer of a righteous person is powerful and effective. God answers. God moves. This is the result we want from our prayers. What makes a righteous person's prayer so powerful and effective?

PRAYING ACCORDING TO GOD'S WILL

Righteous people pray in ways that God wants and will say *yes* to. They've learned to align their desires with God's.

> *This is the confidence we have in approaching God: that if we ask anything according to his will, he hears us. And if we know that he hears us–whatever we ask–we know that we have what we asked of him.* (1 John 5:14-15)

We become vulnerable when we pray according to God's will. Releasing our expectations into His hands is difficult! We're telling God it's okay if He says *no*. That's tough to do. It's all faith. As a parent, I have experienced this frustration when praying for my children and not seeing the results I expected or seeing them on my timetable. Sometimes we only see the results of our prayers in eternity. But God is good; He is still just and still loving. We can trust God, because He keeps His promises.

PRAYING ACCORDING TO GOD'S WORD

Prayer, combined with God's Word, is a powerful weapon, indeed. To be used effectively, we must know God's Word and how it pertains to the situations we are praying for. Sometimes that means searching for what we need. Other times the Holy Spirit leads us to the right verse during our quiet time. Keep a journal handy to jot down these Scriptures as you discover them. Maybe write them on index cards or jot them in a note application on your mobile device–whatever works for you so that you have these ready when you need them.

Let's consider some familiar battles we face and Scriptures that encourage us in them. Are you or is someone you love:

- Feeling alone and/or left out? Find Scriptures that speak to God's presence and His deep love for us. (Hebrews 13:5; 1 John 3:1)

- Not growing in your relationship with God? Paul prayed many prayers for the churches he founded and wrote to. (Philippians 1:9-11)

- In need of salvation? (2 Peter 3:9)

God wants us to pray for all people (1 Timothy 2:1-2). Our parents, spouses, and kids. Our government, our churches, and our schools. We should pray for ourselves, too, and not only when we are in the thick of battle. I think it's easy to gloss over this.

If we don't pray for ourselves, we won't operate at full capacity. The people we love the most won't get the best version of us. They need to see us walking out what we believe during battle. It's easy to *say* we believe certain things, but it's quite another to live it out. This is when our faith has the most power. Others see and can believe there is hope for them, too.

We have God's power when we pray, both offensively and defensively, for ourselves and for others. As we study each piece of the armor, we'll see how the armor of God, the Sword of the Spirit, and our battlefield prayers affect how we live. We'll learn how prayer bolsters our defenses and how it strengthens our offense.

When have you prayed according to God's will and seen God say yes? When has He said no?

_____

_____

_____

_____

_____

day 2

how we pray

And pray in the Spirit on all occasions with all kinds of prayers and requests. With this in mind, be alert and always keep on praying for all the Lord's people. Pray also for me, that whenever I speak, words may be given me so that I will fearlessly make known the mystery of the gospel, for which I am an ambassador in chains. Pray that I may declare it fearlessly, as I should. (EPHESIANS 6:18-20)

In this passage, Paul instructs the Ephesians to pray over everything! In verse 18, we see several inclusive words. We pray on *all* occasions with *all* kinds of prayers and requests. We *always* keep praying for *all* the Lord's people. There are no limits to the prayers we can offer! Paul gives us several ways to pray.

IN THE SPIRIT

The first thing Paul says is to pray in the spirit. When interpreting Scripture, it is essential to keep everything in context. Before we decide what "praying in the Spirit," means, let's look at how Paul refers to the Holy Spirit in Ephesians.

> ***Going Deeper:*** *To find all the places where Paul refers to the Holy Spirit in Ephesians, go to BibleGateway and search for* spirit *in your preferred translation. Once you have your list, filter it for Ephesians only with the options on the right of the screen.*

#standingfirmbiblestudy | 57

week 3 | standing firm in Christ

1. **Read the verses below and underline the Holy Spirit's role in the believer's life.**

   And in him you too are being built together to become a dwelling in which God lives by his Spirit. (Ephesians 2:22)

   I pray that out of his glorious riches he may strengthen you with power through his Spirit in your inner being. (Ephesians 3:16)

   Do not get drunk on wine, which leads to debauchery. Instead, be filled with the Spirit. (Ephesians 5:18)

We will discuss Ephesians 5:18 in more depth when we look at the Breastplate of Righteousness. But for now, it's important to note that being filled with the Spirit means submitting to His leadership in our lives. Remember our study of Ephesians 6:10-20 begins with our three power words. Together, praying in the Spirit is praying under the leadership of the Holy Spirit (according to God's will and His Word), and praying with the power of the Holy Spirit!

WITH FOCUS

Next, we are to be alert (or focused) when we pray. You can't do one thing well when your mind is on something else. In our world of portable devices, it's easy to want to follow up on the text that comes in while you're driving. But you can't drive well while texting. And you can't text well while you're driving. You choose which one you do.

There is a lot to pray for. Honestly, if I prayed for everything on my list at one time, I'm not sure I'd get to anything else I needed to do. Even so, it's easy to get distracted during my prayer time. I've found having something in my hands, such as index cards, helps me stay focused and keeps my mind from wandering.

2. **Write out 1 Peter 5:8. Is it possible to pray when you are not alert and focused on the Lord?**

_____
_____
_____
_____

how we pray | day 2

The night Jesus was betrayed, He took a few of His disciples with Him to a garden to pray. The disciples were not able to focus on prayer because they were tired. In the same way, distractions can keep us from being effective during our prayer time. When we recognize these as our enemy's schemes, we can more easily choose to ignore unimportant interruptions.

PERSISTENTLY

Paul also instructs us to be persistent when we pray, or to pray regularly. But it also means to keep on praying for specific things. Recently my mom (who is a prayer warrior extraordinaire) told me it's easy to wring our hands with worry over the things we pray about. But our job is to pray, pray, and pray some more (1 Thessalonians 5:17). Then we get off our knees, stand up (or stand firm!), and trust God with the outcome. Then we do it all again.

3. **Read Luke 18:1-8 and note what you learn.**

_____

_____

_____

SPECIFICALLY

Approaching the Creator of the universe with our needs is a privilege. God invites us to lift the needs of our friends and families, our churches, our country and its leaders to Him. Through prayer, we get to take part in His work in our world.

> *I urge, then, first of all, that petitions, prayers, intercession and thanksgiving be made for all people–for kings and all those in authority, that we may live peaceful and quiet lives in all godliness and holiness.* (1 Timothy 2:1-2)

Paul told the Ephesians to pray in the Spirit, to be alert, and to pray persistently. While praying for others is essential, we mustn't forget to pray for ourselves. Paul closes this section on prayer by asking the Ephesian church to pray for him.

#standingfirmbiblestudy

week 3 | standing firm in Christ

4. Read the following verses and list the requests Paul makes and the reasons for them.

Ephesians 6:19-20; Romans 15:30-32; Colossians 4:3-4

_____
_____
_____
_____
_____

5. Choose a couple of these verses and identify what else is important about prayer.

John 15:7; James 4:3; 1 John 5:14-15

_____
_____
_____
_____
_____

In the Sermon on the Mount, Jesus explained that God *delights* in meeting our needs. He doesn't lie in wait for an opportunity to cause us harm or to make us feel bad when we approach Him. Instead, He gives us good gifts when we ask Him.

> *Which of you, if your son asks for bread, will give him a stone? Or if he asks for a fish, will give him a snake? If you, then, though you are evil, know how to give good gifts to your children, how much more will your Father in heaven give good gifts to those who ask him!* (Matthew 7:9-11)

day 3

the enemy of prayer

Devote yourselves to prayer, being watchful and thankful. (COLOSSIANS 4:2)

Since prayer is one way God moves in our lives and in the lives of others, we can be assured Satan will do whatever he can to keep us away from it. Today we will look at some ways Satan interferes with our prayer life and Scriptures that show us how we can combat them.

1. **Write out Psalm 66:18. What keeps us from "praying in the spirit"? What do you think the psalmist meant by the word *cherish*?**

   _____
   _____
   _____
   _____
   _____
   _____

Our salvation is never at risk. Our eternity is secure. But unconfessed sin disrupts our relationship with God. Offenses cause rifts in any relationship. The sooner we make things right, the sooner the relationship is back on track. When we have unconfessed sin in our lives, we must confess it. God promises that when we do that, He will cleanse us and restore our relationship with Him.

#standingfirmbiblestudy | 61

week 3 | standing firm in Christ

> *If we confess our sins, he is faithful and just and will forgive us our sins and purify us from all unrighteousness.* (1 John 1:9)

2. According to Matthew 26:36-46, why weren't the disciples able to pray with focus?

_____

_____

_____

    Jesus asked His disciples to keep watch with Him. He also told them to pray so they would not fall into temptation. Jesus knew what was coming and what the disciples needed. However, in their humanity, they slept. As a result, when push came to shove, they were not prepared. Guards came to arrest Jesus and Peter lopped off the ear of one of the High Priest's servants. Jesus immediately healed him. Had that disciple prayed persistently and with focus, he would have been better prepared to handle the situation and not react with hostility.

    We may feel like we don't know how to pray or that our words aren't good enough. Prayer is simply a conversation between you and God, and Jesus gave us a model (Luke 11:1-4). The Apostle Paul prayed all the time. Read any of his letters and you'll find examples of his prayers in the first chapters, for sure.

> ***Going Deeper:*** *Do a BibleGateway search for "I pray" (in quotations) in your preferred translation. Filter your results to* New Testament *and you'll see a nice list of verses where Jesus, Paul, and other writers of Scripture prayed.*

3. Read Psalm 139:1-4 below. What does this tell you about God's knowledge of you and your heart? Note the words *know, perceive, discern,* and *familiar.*

> *You have searched me, LORD, and you know me. You know when I sit and when I rise; you perceive my thoughts from afar. You discern my going out and my lying down; you are familiar with all my ways. Before a word is on my tongue you, LORD, know it completely.* (Psalm 139:1-4)

_____

_____

the enemy of prayer | day 3

God knows us completely. We may think God doesn't understand us, but no one understands us better. He understands what's going on in our minds, and exactly why. Even better, God cares about every detail of our lives, and He wants us to bring them to Him in prayer (1 Peter 5:7).

Some situations in our lives are so painful–a prodigal child, losing a loved one, betrayal. You could add to this list. The emotions that go with these range from deep grief to anger. Our feelings may be intensified as we pray through them. What are we to do?

4. **Read Romans 8:26 and 34. Who is praying when you don't have the words to pray?**

5. **Consider how we pray (from yesterday) and how the enemy's schemes interfere with our effectiveness. What can you do personally to counter this interference?**

Although Jesus gave us a plan for praying, there is no magic formula. The most important thing is to do it. God hears our prayers and sends answers–often before the words leave our mouths (Isaiah 65:24; Matthew 7:7-8). We can sit before Him with all our sorrows, struggles, and anxieties in our hands and lift them to Him as an offering. The Trinity is at work. Jesus Christ and the Holy Spirit petition the Father on our behalf.

day 4

standing firm in prayer

Now it is God who makes both us and you stand firm in Christ. (2 CORINTHIANS 1:21)

Therefore, my dear brothers and sisters, stand firm. Let nothing move you. Always give yourselves fully to the work of the Lord, because you know that your labor in the Lord is not in vain. (1 CORINTHIANS 15:58)

In almost every letter Paul writes, he issues the command to "stand firm." It means to be settled, steady, steadfast, and immovable in mind and purpose.[8] To stand firm in prayer means to be fully committed to prayer, even when circumstances make it difficult. Today we will further our resolve to pray.

1. **Read Colossians 4:2 and Romans 12:12. What are Paul's instructions regarding prayer?**

   _____
   _____
   _____

2. **Read Philippians 4:6-9. How does prayer help us manage worry, and how can you integrate this into your life?**

   _____
   _____
   _____

week 3 | standing firm in Christ

Listed below are some circumstances that threaten our stability. Collecting Scriptures like these sharpens your Sword so you can use it effectively during spiritual warfare. What additional needs and Scriptures can you add to this list?

When we are afraid	Psalm 27:1-2; Psalm 56:3; Isaiah 12:2; John 14:27
When we feel weak or weary	Psalm 9:9; Proverbs 18:10; Ephesians 3:14-21; Matthew 11:28-30
When we are grieving	Psalm 27:13-14; Psalm 139:11-12; Psalm 40:2
When we are broken	Lamentations 3:22-23
When we feel hopeless	Psalm 130 (especially verse 7); Psalm 25:5

3. **For your specific needs, read the verses above, or others you added, and write them into a prayer to help you stand firm.**

   If you are fearful, you could pray something like this, which is based on Psalm 27:1-2.

   Holy Father, You are the light in my darkness, and I cling to You. I have no reason to be afraid, because You are stronger than anything threatening to undo me.

   _____
   _____
   _____
   _____
   _____
   _____
   _____
   _____
   _____
   _____
   _____

Standing firm in prayer is very much a matter of focus. In the Old Testament, God often commanded Israel to move forward, without turning to the right or to the left.

4. Read the following verses and describe how this sense of focus benefited Israel.

Proverbs 4:25-27; Deuteronomy 5:32-33

When the Israelites set the Lord as their focus, they obeyed Him and reaped blessing. But when they took their eyes off the Lord and followed other gods, they experienced defeat. The same is true in prayer. When we focus on the service of praying, we reap blessing. We persist in prayer, even though we don't see the answers we want when we want them. God uses the waiting time to build our faith and trust in Him. He is working, even though we don't see what He's doing. He accomplishes His purpose in our lives and in the lives of those we pray for.

day 5

Prayer is a powerful weapon against our enemy. It's easy to become distracted, but when we focus on Christ, He meets us where we are and uses it to bolster our offense and our defense!

personal action plan

Where do you struggle to pray persistently through your spiritual battles?

_____
_____
_____
_____
_____
_____
_____
_____
_____
_____
_____

Write Scriptures that remind you of the effectiveness of prayer against your enemy.

_____
_____
_____
_____
_____

week 3 | standing firm in Christ

Write a battlefield prayer of commitment to use God's Word in your prayers as you fight your spiritual battles.

Find three songs that strengthen your resolve to pray persistently through your spiritual battles.

week four – the belt of truth

day 1 – the God of truth

day 2 – the belt of truth

day 3 – our enemy is a liar

day 4 – standing firm in the truth

day 5 – personal action plan

week 4 | standing firm in Christ

weekly prep

This week begins our study of the armor of God. Once again, journal about your current battle. Focus on what you *believe* about your spiritual battle. Do you feel defeated? Do you feel alone? Are you transparent in your dealings with people? Are you honest with *yourself* about what's going on in your life? God already knows your struggles. Bringing them into His light will help you stand firm in your battles and find victory. Spill all of it on this page.

day 1

the God of truth

Into your hand I entrust my spirit; you redeem me, LORD, God of truth. (PSALM 31:5, CSB)

I heard a Christian speaker say that everyone lies, including Christians. His statement shocked me. *How could he say that about Christians? Aren't we supposed to be better than this? I mean, I ...*

When I was much younger, I made a sweeping commitment that not one word of untruth would ever pass my lips. For many years I kept that commitment. And then one day ... something changed. I don't remember the exact circumstances. Maybe it was when I let my kids believe in the Tooth Fairy. We never let our kids believe in Santa Claus or the Easter Bunny. (I'm not judging you if you do. This is just my story.) But to let them enjoy the fun to some degree, at Christmas we told them we were Santa. For Easter, we hid eggs for them to find.

It may have been when a telemarketer called. But somewhere along the line, I let a half-truth pass for the absolute truth. When I realized it, I was mortified with myself. Since then, I'm sad to say, occasionally I have not spoken the "complete truth." My guess is that most Christians are like me. Generally, we tell the truth. But "generally" is not God's standard, which should make us feel uncomfortable.

In our culture, "shades of gray" are almost applauded. How many ways can we not tell the truth? Certainly, some things call for discretion. Not everyone involved in a situation needs to know every detail. I'm talking about intentionally covering the truth or trying to make the truth look better than what it is.

But what is truth?

#standingfirmbiblestudy

Truth is what is real. It's the fact of how things are. Our God is the *One true God*. He is real. Everything He says is true. He is who He says He is. Throughout Scripture He tells us this:

> *For this is what the L*ORD *says–he who created the heavens, he is God; he who fashioned and made the earth, he founded it; he did not create it to be empty, but formed it to be inhabited–he says: "I am the L*ORD*, and there is no other."* (Isaiah 45:18)

GOD IS TRUTH

Themes of truth run strong and clear through God's Word. Let's look at Psalm 31:5 in a couple of translations.

> *Into your hand I entrust my spirit; you have redeemed me, L*ORD*, God of truth.*
> *(Psalm 31:5, CSB)*

> *Into your hands I commit my spirit; deliver me, L*ORD*, my faithful God.* (Psalm 31:5, NIV)

The Hebrew word for truth, ***emet***, is sometimes translated *wholeheartedly, faithful, honor, loyal, secure,* or *pure*. Psalm 31:5 gives us a beautiful Name of God. When paired with *el* (which means *God*), we have:

> ***el emet***: THE GOD OF TRUTH

Truth is one aspect of God's nature. In the same way that God is love, He is also truth. Truth does not exist outside of Him. Truth is who He is. *The Complete Word Study Dictionary of the Old Testament* further defines ***emet***:

> It is frequently connected with lovingkindness and occasionally with other terms such as peace, righteousness, and justice. To walk in truth is to conduct oneself according to God's holy standards. Truth was the barometer for measuring both one's word and actions. Accordingly, God's words and actions are characterized by this Hebrew term as well. Indeed, God is the only God of truth.[9]

Moses's first encounter with God was dramatic. As he spent time in God's presence and followed His commands, their relationship became increasingly intimate. One day Moses asked God:

You have been telling me, "Lead these people," but you have not let me know whom you will send with me. You have said, "I know you by name and you have found favor with me." If you are pleased with me, teach me your ways so I may know you and continue to find favor with you. Remember that this nation is your people. (Exodus 33:12-13)

> **Going Deeper:** *Do a BibleGateway search in the NIV with the phrase "there is no other" (use quotation marks). What other phrases can you think of that might bring up related passages? Try them out. See what you find.*

Moses wanted to know God's ways so He could understand Him better and continue to enjoy His favor. God answered that prayer with a *yes*. God tucked Moses into the crevice of a rock so he could look on His glory. When God walked by, Moses saw His back. Then God called out His Own Name:

And he passed in front of Moses, proclaiming, "The LORD, the LORD, the compassionate and gracious God, slow to anger, abounding in love and faithfulness." (Exodus 34:6)

In this verse, *faithfulness* is **emet**. After years of Moses's following God closely, God gave him a song. He told him to write it down and teach it to the Israelites. The song proclaims the character of God and how He cared for His people, despite their rebellion. He opens with these beautiful words:

Listen, you heavens, and I will speak ... I will proclaim the name of the LORD. Oh, praise the greatness of our God! He is the Rock, his works are perfect, and all his ways are just. A faithful God who does no wrong, upright and just is he. (Deuteronomy 32:1-4)

Have you ever been dishonest with yourself? It's a miserable place to live. Deep inside, you know the truth, but you ignore it. All the while, God's hand is heavy, convicting you of the truth. Sometimes we might peek at the truth and turn away. We know that if we admit the truth, we are accountable for our actions and their result in light of that truth. We're not ready for genuine heart change. We think that returning to God will be too painful. The truth is, abandoning our sin and turning toward God is the most freeing thing ever.

David's Example

King David is known for being a "man after God's own heart" (1 Samuel 13:14). Unfortunately, he is also known for adultery and murder (2 Samuel 11). He ignored God's conviction for an entire year. When he finally repented of his sin, he wrote Psalms 32 and 51, which show us the way back to a restored relationship with God.

Surely you desire integrity in the inner self, and you teach me wisdom deep within.
(Psalm 51:6, CSB)

Truth in our inner self is being completely honest with ourselves. It's not intellectual assent. It's not avoiding discovery or disclosure. It's coming into complete agreement with God. When we refuse to acknowledge truth, like David, we can expect disastrous results. He was utterly depressed, and his body wasted away. Most significantly, he experienced disruption in his intimacy with God.

> Abandoning our sin and turning toward God is the most freeing thing ever.

God wants us to lay it all out before Him, not covering anything up (Psalm 32:5). The result is beautiful. When we confess our sins, God forgives our sins (Psalm 32:5; 1 John 1:9). Our relationship with God is restored. Once again, we hear His voice of instruction and experience His protection. No longer are our hearts weighed down with sin. Instead, we are free to rejoice from a pure heart.

GOD'S WAY

The Book of Proverbs is a mini manual for successful living. It contains instructions on a myriad of topics–including honesty. Consequences arise when we lie or compromise our integrity. When we tell "shades of truth," we sabotage our relationships. Because God loves us, He tells us straight up what pitfalls lie ahead when we choose dishonesty. God is against all who are dishonest, but He pours His favor on those who walk in integrity.

God detests every kind of untruth: deception (Proverbs 8:7), lying (Proverbs 6:17; 12:22), inaccurate scales and measures (Proverbs 11:1; Proverbs 20:10, 23).

God's way of living (being honest with everyone, in every situation), is a place of strength, safety, and security (Proverbs 10:20). He delights in those who tell the truth (Proverbs 11:20; 12:22).

Reading through the Book of Proverbs shows the consequences of deceptive living and the rewards for walking in integrity. Eventually, lies are exposed, but truth stands the test of time

(Proverbs 12:19). Truth is a hallmark of God's character. In a culture where "shades of gray" are often the rule, God wants our lives to shine His clear light of truth. And it begins in our own hearts.

JESUS IS THE TRUTH

In the same way that God is truth, Jesus is truth. Throughout his gospel, John explains the power of truth in Jesus's life. Right away John sets the stage.

> *The Word became flesh and made his dwelling among us. We have seen his glory, the glory of the one and only Son, who came from the Father, full of grace and truth.*
> (John 1:14)

Jesus is the Word of God made flesh–*full* of grace and truth. Consider a full glass of water. There isn't room for anything else. Jesus is full of truth. It is the core of His being. Truth is who He is. Any time Jesus said, "I tell you the truth," He either taught a timeless truth or corrected a false teaching. The Pharisees misinterpreted the Law and forced Israel to carry the weight of meticulous obedience. Jesus exposed these lies and presented beautiful, freeing truth.

In John 6, Jesus fed five thousand men, along with their families. They had been following Jesus, the day was getting long, and the crowd was hungry. No one except a young boy packed a lunch. Jesus used his five loaves of bread and two fish to feed all of them. The following day, the crowd found Jesus and asked Him what *works* God required of them (verse 28). Recognizing that they were focused on the *miracle* instead of *the message* of the miracle, Jesus corrected their thinking.

They had been taught that *Moses* provided manna in the wilderness. In reality, it was *God the Father* who provided the manna. First, Jesus explained that the "work" God required was for them to believe that He was God's Son and was sent by Him (verse 29). Then He told them this:

> *Jesus said to them, "Very truly I tell you, it is not Moses who has given you the bread from heaven, but it is my Father who gives you the true bread from heaven. For the bread of God is the bread that comes down from heaven and gives life to the world."*
> (John 6:32-33)

Jesus wanted them to get it right. As long as they misunderstood (thinking Moses gave the bread), they missed being fed from the Bread of Life Himself–and having eternal life!

> *Very truly I tell you, the one who believes has eternal life. I am the bread of life. Your ancestors ate the manna in the wilderness, yet they died. But here is the bread that comes down from heaven, which anyone may eat and not die.* (John 6:47-50)

SPIRIT OF TRUTH

The night before Jesus was crucified, He promised His disciples that God would send the Holy Spirit to replace His physical presence on earth after He ascended into heaven (John 14:16). As a result, the Holy Spirit indwells every believer at the moment of salvation and helps us understand the truth in God's Word. Unbelievers, who don't have the Holy Spirit, can't understand spiritual things until they are born again (1 Corinthians 2:13-14).

The Holy Spirit also imparts truth when we need it (John 14:26). When we are lonely, He reminds us that God never leaves us or forsakes us (Hebrews 13:5). When we face temptation, the Holy Spirit reminds us that we belong to God and are not slaves to sin (Romans 6:6)–meaning that sin does not have control over us. Any time we feel "less than," or unworthy, the Holy Spirit reminds us that yes, we are unworthy–but God loves us still. He knows our weaknesses but delights in us anyway (Zephaniah 3:17).

The Holy Spirit also helps us discern truth from error. John knew that many false teachers would try to deceive us (1 John 4:1-6). They were prevalent when he wrote his letters. They are prevalent today. As a result of our studying God's Word, when false teachers present themselves, the Holy Spirit helps us recognize what is true and what is not.

> ***Going Deeper:*** *Do a BibleGateway search for "spirit of truth" (in quotes or not, try it both ways) to see all the places the Spirit of Truth is mentioned.*

Whatever we build our lives on influences the ways we think, feel, speak, and act.

The Truth of God's Word is the foundation for our Christian faith. When we fully engage with God's Word and build our lives on its truth, the Holy Spirit will bring it to our minds in our moments of need. We will recognize the enemy's lies and not fall prey to his schemes.

> *We demolish arguments and every pretension that sets itself up against the knowledge of God, and we take captive every thought to make it obedient to Christ.* (2 Corinthians 10:5)

day 2

the belt of truth

Stand firm then, with the belt of truth buckled around your waist, with the breastplate of righteousness in place. (EPHESIANS 6:14)

When a Roman soldier prepared for battle, he fastened a leather belt over his tunic and around his waist. He attached his weapons to thick leather straps that hung from the belt. This "belt" protected his loins and kept his tunic in place so he could move around freely, all while keeping his weapons within easy grasp.

2 Kings 4:8-37 tells the story of a Shunammite woman. She and her husband prepared a guest room for the prophet Elisha to stay in when he was in their area. She could not bear children. As a thank you for her kindness, Elisha worked a miracle so she could. Soon after that, she had a son. Several years later, her son died. Immediately she traveled to where Elisha was to tell him about her son. Elisha gave his servant his staff and sent him to the boy with instructions to lay the staff on the boy and he would be healed. But before he left, Elisha said, "Tuck your cloak into your belt … and run" (2 Kings 4:29). Soldiers were not the only ones who wore belts. The belt kept the servant's cloak out of the way so he could run unhindered.

The Belt of Truth provides similar protection. At its core, the Belt of Truth is being honest. *The Bible Knowledge Commentary* says it this way:

> As a soldier's belt or sash gave ease and freedom of movement, so truth gives freedom with self, others, and God.[10]

week 4 | standing firm in Christ

We all want and need this kind of freedom in our lives. Parents work hard to build this character trait into their children. We teach them that a life of honesty is much simpler. People who lie, especially those who build complicated stories, have a lot to remember. Eventually the truth comes out, along with the repercussions of their falsehood.

1. **Read Ephesians 4:25 and Colossians 3:9. What are we to "put off"?**

   _____
   _____
   _____

2. **Read Leviticus 19:11-13 and underline each instance that refers to falsehood.**

   Do not steal. Do not lie. Do not deceive one another. Do not swear falsely by my name and so profane the name of your God. I am the LORD. Do not defraud or rob your neighbor. Do not hold back the wages of a hired worker overnight.
   (Leviticus 19:11-13)

   God wants His people to live above reproach, with no hint of falsehood. This includes everything we think, speak, and do. Jesus confronts the problem of hypocrisy among the Pharisees, a part of Israel's religious ruling class.

3. **Read Matthew 23:1-7. What was the motive behind the Pharisees' actions?**

   _____
   _____
   _____

4. **Read Psalm 15. Write out Proverbs 11:3. Summarize what you learn about integrity.**

   _____
   _____
   _____
   _____

Sometimes speaking the truth means confronting a loved one with his or her actions. Paul gives specific instructions regarding this.

5. Read Ephesians 4:15 below and underline how Paul says we are to speak truth.

Instead, speaking the truth in love, we will grow to become in every respect the mature body of him who is the head, that is, Christ. (Ephesians 4:15)

Telling the truth, confessing our sins to those we've hurt and asking for forgiveness, and confronting a loved one with the truth of their actions are all part of living a life of integrity. Standing firm in truth is not easy, and it does not give us a license to be unkind. Living in truth includes living from a heart of love.

day 3

our enemy is a liar

The devil ... was a murderer from the beginning, not holding to the truth, for there is no truth in him. When he lies, he speaks his native language, for he is a liar and the father of lies. (JOHN 8:44)

Jesus constantly faced opposition from the Jewish ruling elite. The Pharisees criticized everything He said and did. They, along with His disciples, scorned Jesus when He ate dinner with unseemly characters and were surprised when He showed kindness toward the outcasts of society. They accused Him of violating the Law when He healed people on the Sabbath and were humiliated when Jesus chose to forgive instead of stone a woman caught in adultery.

But Jesus was a truth-teller. Throughout the gospels, Jesus corrects the false teaching fostered by the Pharisees. Which, you guessed it, infuriated them even further. After one such encounter, Jesus explained that since they didn't recognize Him as the Son of God, they must be children of the devil, whom Jesus nick-named him "the father of lies" (John 8:44).

Satan's goal is to thwart God's plan at every turn. From the beginning of time, his strategy has been to lie and convince us his lies are truth.

> ***Going Deeper****: Look up Genesis 12:10-20 on BibleGateway. Be sure the STUDY pane is open, and scroll to the bottom. Click on THE DICTIONARY OF BIBLE THEMES. Scroll to the bottom again, and click on "8776 lies." This will bring up many categories of Scriptures related to lies.*

#standingfirmbiblestudy | 83

week 4 | standing firm in Christ

1. Why do you think we lie?

_____

_____

_____

When we lie, we say that we don't trust God. For example, God promised Abraham that He would make a great nation out of him. But when faced with a situation that might cost him his life, he did not trust God. Instead, he lied to protect himself (Genesis 12). Abraham's lie did not thwart God's plan. Although there were still consequences from Abraham's lie, God was merciful and worked around it.

God is sovereign, and His purposes will always stand. That doesn't mean we won't face the consequences of our sin. Sometimes our lies shift the trajectory of our lives and those around us. They hurt the ones we love; they hurt us, and they destroy our hope for trust-filled, wholesome relationships.

Sometimes we lie to ourselves. Such was the case with King David. 2 Samuel 11 tells the story of his sin with Bathsheba. It took almost a year before David confessed his sin. During that time, David suffered the inescapable result of hiding his sin from God. He penned Psalm 32 and Psalm 51, which describes his path to repentance.

2. What does David mean by the phrase "in whose spirit is no deceit"?

> *Blessed is the one whose transgressions are forgiven, whose sins are covered. Blessed is the one whose sin the LORD does not count against them and in whose spirit is no deceit.* (Psalm 32:1-2)

_____

_____

_____

_____

our enemy is a liar | day 3

3. Read Psalm 32:3-4. While David "lied to himself," what else did he experience?

_____
_____
_____
_____

4. Read the rest of Psalm 32, and describe the result of David's repentance.

_____
_____
_____
_____
_____

Although it may be true that "everyone lies," we deceive ourselves if we believe this to be an acceptable part of the Christian's life.

5. Read Proverbs 6:16-19 below, and underline how God feels about truth, honesty, and lies.

*There are six things the LORD hates, seven that are detestable to him: haughty eyes, **a lying tongue**, hands that shed innocent blood, a heart that devises wicked schemes, feet that are quick to rush into evil, **a false witness who pours out lies** and a person who stirs up conflict in the community.* (Proverbs 6:16-19, emphasis added)

Did you catch that? Of the seven things the Lord detests, He mentions lying twice. Throughout Scripture, our God of Truth emphasizes the importance He places on truth.

- The ninth commandment states that we are not to lie about our neighbors in court (Exodus 20:16).

- Proverbs tells us that God detests a lying tongue (Proverbs 6:16-17; 12:22).

- Paul instructed the church members at Colossae not to lie to each other. Lying is part of our old nature. Once we become believers in Christ, the Holy Spirit resides in us, giving us a new nature (Colossians 3:9).

#standingfirmbiblestudy | 85

There is nothing quite as refreshing as having someone you can count on to speak the truth.

6. **Do you know anyone who does not lie? At all? Who are they? Describe them and how their integrity affects you.**

___
___
___
___
___
___
___
___
___
___

day 4

standing firm in the truth

Jesus answered, "I am the way and the truth and the life. No one comes to the Father except through me." (JOHN 14:6)

Yesterday we learned that Satan is a liar. He lied to Eve and caused her to doubt what God said. God's instructions were simple: Don't eat from the tree of the knowledge of good and evil. Eat from the tree of life. But after encountering the serpent Eve chose to eat from the tree of the knowledge of good and evil (Genesis 3). Since then, Satan has woven his lies into the fabric of history. Sometimes his lies are blatant. Other times they are subtle. If Adam and Eve had believed God's truth, they would have experienced life. Instead, they believed the lies of Satan–and physical and spiritual death were born.

Truth brings LIFE. Lies bring DEATH.

1. **Read John 1:14-17. What do these verses say about who Jesus is and what He embodies?**

_____
_____
_____

Jesus was born into our world fully human. He experienced everything we experience physically, emotionally, and mentally. But He was also fully God. The fullness of God's character and His divine power dwelled within Jesus's earthly body (Colossians 2:9). The big theological word for this is *incarnation*. It means that Jesus was fully God and fully man–at the same time.

week 4 | standing firm in Christ

Jesus's purpose in coming to earth was to reveal the truth. Satan had confused Israel's idea of what it meant to draw close to God. The Jewish religious leaders added meticulous details to the Mosaic Law, which was already complicated. In so doing, they overburdened the Jews of that day. Throughout the gospels, Jesus corrected these inaccurate teachings by shining the light of truth on them.

Jesus's continual correcting drove these Jewish leaders crazy. They became so angry, they wanted Jesus eliminated, but they had no legal authority to convict and sentence Him. Once they arrested Jesus, they took Him before the Roman governor, Pontius Pilate, who did have power to convict and condemn. Jesus and Pilate had an interesting conversation. I wish we were privy to all its details.

Read the passage below.

> Then [the Jewish leaders] led Jesus from Caiaphas to the governor's headquarters. It was early morning. They did not enter the headquarters themselves; otherwise they would be defiled and unable to eat the Passover. So Pilate came out to them and said, "What charge do you bring against this man?" They answered him, "If this man weren't a criminal, we wouldn't have handed him over to you." Pilate told them, "You take him and judge him according to your law." "It's not legal for us to put anyone to death," the Jews declared. They said this so that Jesus's words might be fulfilled indicating what kind of death he was going to die. Then Pilate went back into the headquarters, summoned Jesus, and said to him, "Are you the king of the Jews?" Jesus answered, "Are you asking this on your own, or have others told you about me?" "I'm not a Jew, am I?" Pilate replied. "Your own nation and the chief priests handed you over to me. What have you done?" "My kingdom is not of this world," said Jesus. "If my kingdom were of this world, my servants would fight, so that I wouldn't be handed over to the Jews. But as it is, my kingdom is not from here." "You are a king then?" Pilate asked. "You say that I'm a king," Jesus replied. "I was born for this, and I have come into the world for this: to testify to the truth. Everyone who is of the truth listens to my voice." "What is truth?" said Pilate. (John 18:28-38a, CSB)

2. **How does Jesus answer Pilate about why He came into the world?**

_____

_____

3. **Just a few hours before this encounter, Jesus told His disciples that He was the way, the truth, and the life. Read John 14:1-6. According to these verses, what do you understand each of them to mean?**

The way:

_____

_____

The truth:

_____

_____

The life:

_____

_____

The gospel truth: Jesus is the only way to the Father, in whom we experience eternal life.

4. **Read John 8:32 and Romans 6:5-7. How does the truth set us free?**

_____

_____

_____

Jesus is truth. He shines light into darkness so we can know when our enemy is trying to deceive us and when he wants us to doubt what God has said. But when we build our lives on the truth of God's Word (our sword!) and stand firm in Christ, we will discern truth from error.

> ***Going Deeper:*** *Do separate BibleGateway searches for* true *and* truth *in the NIV. Note the number of occurrences in the Gospel of John as compared to the other gospels.*
> *Do a BibleGateway search for* truly *in the NIV. Note the number of occurrences in the gospels. Most of the time, when we see the phrase "Truly I tell you" Jesus is correcting a*

day 5

We wear the Belt of Truth when we build our lives on the truth of God's Word, which influences the ways we think, feel, speak, and act. So established, we stand firm in Christ and discern truth from error.

personal action plan

Jesus Christ is the way, the truth, and the life. In Christ, you wear truth like a garment. It is the foundation of your life. Refer to what you journaled on Day 1. Do you struggle with personal integrity? Do you need to make any adjustments to what you *believe to be true* about your spiritual battle? If so, journal that here.

_____
_____
_____
_____
_____
_____

What Scriptures counter any lies you may have believed?

_____
_____
_____
_____
_____
_____
_____

week 4 | standing firm in Christ

Using the verses you chose, write a battlefield prayer of commitment.

Find three songs that challenge you to stand firm in truth.

week five – the breastplate of righteousness

day 1 – the God of righteousness

day 2 – the breastplate of righteousness

day 3 – our enemy exploits our weaknesses

day 4 – standing firm in Christ's righteousness

day 5 – personal action plan

week 5 | standing firm in Christ

weekly prep

This week we study the breastplate of righteousness. We will learn that everything we do stems from what's in our hearts. Consider the spiritual battle you currently face. How do you feel toward the people or elements involved in your battle? Be honest. (Remember that your life is founded on truth!) What do you love, and what do you hate? Maybe hate is too strong a word. What (or whom) in your battle causes you the greatest frustration?

_____
_____
_____
_____
_____
_____
_____
_____
_____
_____
_____
_____
_____
_____
_____
_____
_____

day 1

the God of righteousness

"The days are coming," declares the LORD, "when I will raise up for David a righteous Branch, a King who will reign wisely and do what is just and right in the land. In his days Judah will be saved and Israel will live in safety. This is the name by which he will be called: The LORD Our Righteous Savior." (JEREMIAH 23:5-6)

R ighteousness is "right living." It's right thinking, right feeling, right speaking, right behavior. It's "right *everything*"! Righteousness stems from a *heart* that is right. For everything we say and do springs forth from our hearts (Proverbs 4:23). Only God is righteous. It is the core of His being. Everything He does, He does righteously. It is also the standard God set for us.

For the LORD is righteous, he loves justice; the upright will see his face. (Psalm 11:7)

In the Old Testament, this standard was known as "The Law." Its purpose was multifold. It helped the Israelites understand right from wrong and the consequences for disobedience. Most importantly, however, it showed Israel what God's righteousness and holiness looked like–and how far they were from it. God required atonement (or a payment) for unrighteousness. The sacrificial system was a part of The Law's provision for this. At various times throughout the year, people brought perfect, first-born animals (from doves to goats and bulls) to the priests. When the people killed these animals according to God's detailed instructions, the blood atoned for (or covered) their sins. God no longer requires the blood of animals for the forgiveness of sin. Jesus Christ's death, burial, and resurrection satisfies God's requirement for a perfect sacrifice, but God still expects us to pursue a righteous life.

#standingfirmbiblestudy

OUR RIGHTEOUS GOD (a brief history)

God uses family relationships to describe His relationship with Israel. Sometimes He uses the image of a father to show His nurturing, protective nature (Deuteronomy 1:31; Psalm 68:5; Romans 8:15). Most often, however, God uses the love and fidelity between husband and wife to describe His relationship with Israel (Isaiah 54:5). This metaphor is carried into the New Testament, identifying the Church as the Bride and Jesus as the Bridegroom.

Fidelity and trust are paramount in spousal relationships. Few marriages can withstand infidelity. Neither can marriages be strong when trust is absent. If you have been the victim of infidelity, you understand the heartache God feels when we choose other people or things over Him. You also understand if you have a spouse who isn't trustworthy.

Looking through the lens of a parent or a spouse while reading through the Old Testament, we gain a better understanding of God's heart when we see Israel abandon Him. It's how He feels when we choose not to follow Him, as well.

The nation of Israel was united under the reigns of her first three kings: Saul, David, and Solomon. David was the "good king" God provided for them. He was known as a "man after God's own heart" (1 Samuel 13:14).

After Solomon's reign, however, Israel split into two nations. The Southern Kingdom (which included the tribes of Benjamin and Judah) was named *Judah*. The Northern Kingdom (which included the remaining ten tribes) retained the name *Israel*.

Subsequent kings (even Solomon) drew Israel away from God. Occasionally other "good kings" would come to power. They kept the nation's focus on God, but it never lasted. Eventually Israel and Judah abandoned their faith for good and adopted the evil religious practices of their neighboring countries.

During these years of rebellion, God sent prophets instructing Israel and Judah to repent of their wickedness and return to Him. If they didn't, judgment would come. Jeremiah 23 condemns the wicked kings and their ineffectiveness at shepherding God's people. However, God promised a good Shepherd who would care for His children.

> *"The days are coming," declares the LORD, "when I will raise up for David a righteous Branch, a King who will reign wisely and do what is just and right in the land. In his days Judah will be saved and Israel will live in safety. This is the name by which he will be called: The LORD Our Righteous Savior."* (Jeremiah 23:5-6)

The "righteous branch" in verse 5 refers to Jesus Christ–the promised Messiah. Unlike the unrighteous kings, Jesus is a righteous King. He partially fulfilled this prophecy at His first coming. As New Testament believers, we receive His righteousness.

yahweh tsidqenuw: THE LORD OUR RIGHTEOUSNESS

The prophet Isaiah also called the nation to repentance and prophesied about the coming Messiah. Judah saw the Northern Kingdom (Israel) invaded by the Assyrians and be destroyed. Judah was warned that the same disaster would befall them if they did not repent and return to their righteous God.

But Judah did not repent. Approximately two hundred years later, Nebuchadnezzar laid siege to Jerusalem, destroyed the temple, and took the Israelites captive. Judah was forced to relocate from Jerusalem to Babylon. It would be seventy years before they returned to their homes. During exile, an entire generation died, leaving the next generation with little knowledge of the One True God.

Isaiah describes Israel as a vineyard, with Judah holding a special place in God's heart. He found the perfect place on the side of a hill and prepared the soil just so. He removed stones and weeds and turned the soil so it would receive the plants well. Then He chose the best vines and planted them. He put a watchtower and a winepress in the vineyard and expected a great crop. He did everything a Master Gardener would do to make sure His crop was bountiful. God's desire was for them to be fruitful, to provide nourishment for other nations, and to reflect His righteousness. But when He went to harvest the grapes, they were bad. Israel had followed pagan cultures and Baal worship. Polytheism and Greek mythology had taken root by this time, so it's likely they had embraced these practices as well.

God asked, "What more could I have done?" He did everything He could for Israel to follow Him and to be a light to the nations. Because of Israel's rebellion, He removed all the protection He had built. He allowed the vineyard to be trampled on and for rocks and weeds to take over once again (Isaiah 5:1-7). As punishment, God allowed her to fall into ruin and be taken captive by other nations.

In Isaiah's call for repentance, he reminds Judah of the righteous God they abandoned.

> *There is no God apart from me, **a righteous God** and a Savior; there is none but me.*
> (Isaiah 45:21, emphasis added)

One day, God's chosen people will be everything He wants them to be. When Jesus returns to earth, Israel will return to God and be a picture of His righteousness. Isaiah describes them as "oaks of righteousness, a planting of the LORD for the display of his splendor" (Isaiah 61:3).

God's Standard

God proclaims His righteousness throughout Scripture. We are like children who forget and need reminders. We may think, *Yeah, I know God is righteous. He's God.* But if we *really knew,* how would that impact the way we live?

> ***Going Deeper:*** *Do a BibleGateway search with the words* God *and* Righteous *in the search field. Do another one with* Lord *and* Righteous. *As you skim these verses, do you see any repeated phrases you might like to search out on your own? Try* "righteousness endures forever" *in quotations. How does this add to your understanding?*

Righteousness is the standard God requires of His children. In and of ourselves, there is no way we can reach that standard. Our hearts are wicked (Jeremiah 17:9). A quick scan of the front page of any media outlet shows how wicked our society is. Sex, lust, and all forms of depravity are at our fingertips daily.

We may think those stories are not about *us*. No sirree. *We* are "good people." We're not stuck in that stuff. We are good people who take pride in our own goodness, especially when we compare ourselves to those around us. But the Bible has something to say about that, too. No matter how good we may think we are, our "righteousness" is like a filthy rag (Isaiah 64:6). Although our attempts at righteousness are futile, God made a way for us to become righteous in His sight.

Jesus is Our Righteousness

The Pharisees and the Sadducees were the religious leaders of Jesus's day. The Pharisees studied the Law of Moses in detail and were responsible for teaching Israel what God expected. Problem was, they added more rules to God's Law, creating a heavy burden for them to bear.

Jesus shined the light of truth on the lies of the Pharisees. They asked Him which commandment was the greatest. Jesus explained that the true Law depended on loving God and loving others. He said:

> *Love the Lord your God with all your heart and with all your soul and with all your mind. This is the first and greatest commandment. And the second is like it: Love your neighbor as yourself. All the Law and the Prophets* **hang** *on these two commandments.*
> (Matthew 22:37-40, emphasis added)

Interestingly, the word *hang* is related to ***histēmi***, our word for *stand*. Consider this:

The Law is established, or built, on the two commands
to love God and to love others.

When we love God with all our hearts, we don't worship idols. When we treasure God's Name, we don't misuse it. When we truly love others, we don't steal from them, or desire anything that belongs to them. We wouldn't dream of hurting them physically or in any other way. This is the message Jesus taught. We express our love for God and others in how we treat them.

The Old Testament makes clear that God's righteousness is the only standard by which Israel was to live. The Law showed Israel that they were incapable of living up to God's standard. He required them to shed the blood of perfect, innocent animals to pay for the guilt of their sin.

The New Testament echoes this teaching. The good news is that Jesus, God's perfect Son, is the fulfillment of the Law. He was born to a young virgin woman and lived a sinless life. He experienced temptation (especially when He was vulnerable), just like we do (Matthew 4).

Yet He did not sin (Hebrews 4:15). Jesus *lived perfectly*, and He *loved perfectly*. Though He wronged no one, He suffered and died a criminal's death. Jesus's death on the cross satisfied God's requirement of a perfect blood sacrifice for the penalty of sin. As such, the sacrificial system of the Old Testament is no longer needed (Hebrews 10:9-10).

Because of our unrighteousness, eternal death (separation from God) is still the wage (what we earn) for our sin. Jesus experienced separation from His Father on our behalf when He died on the cross. When we receive this Gift by faith, we become God's children and are granted salvation from sin (or death) and will spend eternity with Him.

It's a beautiful exchange. Jesus paid the penalty for our sin so we could receive His righteousness and have eternal life.

> *This righteousness is given through faith in Jesus Christ to all who believe. There is no difference between Jew and Gentile.* (Romans 3:22)

Becoming a child of God (accepting Jesus as Savior or being born again) does not make us perfect. Nor does it remove God's requirement for how we live our lives. In fact, when we look at our righteous God, we see ourselves rightly.

God still requires us to live righteously. It's a struggle, because our old sin nature wars with our new spirit nature. Even the Ten Commandments are difficult to keep. On the surface they may seem simple. But live for a few minutes, and we may discover ourselves wishing life could be like someone else's. We might even crave something more than the life-giving Word of God. With these, we've broken the tenth commandment: You shall not covet.

How then, are we to live righteously?

SPIRIT OF RIGHTEOUSNESS

On our own, it is impossible to live the righteous life God requires. Even as believers, we fall short in our efforts to meet God's requirement. God gave us the Holy Spirit to help us understand the truth in Scripture. He also gave us the Holy Spirit, who gives us the power to live righteously, as we grow in our faith. It gets down to one question:

Who is in control of our lives?

Paul told the Ephesian church not to be drunk with wine, but instead to be filled with the Holy Spirit (Ephesians 5:18). Do you ever wonder why Paul related drinking wine (or being drunk) with being filled with the Spirit? Paul used alcohol as a metaphor to describe that *we choose* what controls our lives. Alcohol dulls our senses. Continuing to drink makes alcohol a taskmaster. "Responsible drinkers" stay home rather than drink and drive, thus missing many delightful things that occur after working hours, such as fellowship with other believers or our children's activities. Stuck at home with the TV, we may think we control the alcohol; in fact, it controls us. Ultimately, unsatisfied cravings lead to irritability. (Ask me how I know! I struggled with this for many years, until I finally yielded to God's direction for my life.)

> The more we surrender to the Holy Spirit, the more power He gives us to live a life of victory. We are not bound by the power of sin because we live in the power of the Spirit.

This is not what Paul had in mind. We want the Holy Spirit to control our lives–not anything else. How does this occur?

Being filled with the Spirit is a conscious yielding of our will to God's will. Sometimes we want things that aren't necessarily bad. They just aren't what God wants for us now. When we yield to the Holy Spirit, we choose God's best over other "good" things.

As we grow in our faith, "spiritual fruit" becomes evident in our lives (Galatians 5:22-23). Instead of hating, we love. We find joy when most people grumble. Peace instead of anxiety rules our hearts and minds. Kindness and goodness define our actions. We are faithful instead of fickle. Gentle instead of caustic. Our passions don't rule our lives.

> *And this is my prayer: that…you may be…filled with the fruit of righteousness that comes through Jesus Christ–to the glory and praise of God.* (Philippians 1:9-11)

What about when we mess up? When we let our passions and desires get the best of us? Again, God has a plan.

> *If we confess our sins, he is faithful and just and will forgive us our sins and purify us from all unrighteousness.* (1 John 1:9)

Did you catch that? God's forgiveness **purifies** us from all unrighteousness. When God looks at us, He doesn't see what we see. He sees us as righteous. The more we surrender to the Holy Spirit, the more power He gives us to live a life of victory. We are not bound by the power of sin because we live in the power of the Spirit.

> *God made him who had no sin to be sin for us, so that in him we might become the righteousness of God.* (2 Corinthians 5:21)

Consider who is in control of your life. Are you fully submitted to the Holy Spirit's leadership? Write a prayer of commitment.

_____
_____
_____
_____
_____
_____
_____
_____

day 2

the breastplate of righteousness

Stand firm then, with the belt of truth buckled around your waist, with the breastplate of righteousness in place. (EPHESIANS 6:14)

With the belt buckled snuggly around his waist, the Roman soldier then put on his body armor–or breastplate. It covered his chest, his back, and all his vital organs, including his heart. What does the heart have to do with righteousness?

Above all else, guard your heart, for everything you do flows from it. (Proverbs 4:23)

1. **Let's ask some basic questions. According to Proverbs 4:23:**

What is the first thing Solomon says?

_____

Why do you think he prefaces his instructions with this phrase?

_____
_____
_____

#standingfirmbiblestudy |103

week 5 | standing firm in Christ

What is the core (or heart) of this Proverb?
_____

What does it mean to "guard your heart"?
_____
_____

Why does Solomon tell us to guard our hearts?
_____
_____

Can you think of a personal example of how your heart affects something you do?
_____
_____
_____
_____

We manifest what is in our hearts with our words and actions. Throughout the Gospels, Jesus talks about the relationship between what is in our hearts and how we think, act, and speak.

2. **Read Matthew 15:10-20. What does Jesus tell the crowds about the heart?**
_____
_____
_____

Apart from Christ's saving work, our hearts are wicked (Jeremiah 17:9). When we read about Israel in the Old Testament, it's easy to think we are better than they. After all, they turned their backs on God over and over. But the truth is, had we been the Israelites, we would have done the same thing. God didn't choose Israel because they were unique and full of potential. Israel was unique and full of potential—*because God chose them*.

Isaiah 59 describes the sin and rebellion that characterized the nation of Israel. They were so depraved that no one could save them. But God saw their oppression and explained that *He* was strong and able to save Israel. Even though their sin had separated them from Him, *He* stepped in.

> *He was appalled that there was no one to intervene; so his own arm achieved salvation for him, and his own righteousness sustained him. He put on righteousness as his breastplate, and the helmet of salvation on his head; he put on the garments of vengeance and wrapped himself in zeal as in a cloak.* (Isaiah 59:16-17)

Think about this for a minute. God sees you and every sin you've committed. He sees the attitude of your heart and your resistance to obey Him. Maybe you're so deep in sin that no one can help you. Not your best friend, your parents, or your spouse. You are alone in your sin.

But love…the verses above describe how God, in His own righteousness, arms Himself for battle and steps in. He fights for you! This is what God did to rescue you from sin and darkness. The whole chapter is beautiful and points to Jesus Christ as our ultimate salvation.

3. Read 2 Corinthians 5:20-21. God stepped in. What did He do on your behalf?

_____

_____

_____

4. Write out 2 Corinthians 3:18, and emphasize God's primary purpose for believers.

_____

_____

_____

God sent Jesus to provide righteousness for us. Jesus lived a perfect life and paid the penalty for our sin. But we have a part in this as well.

5. **Read Romans 4:4-5 below, and underline how we obtain righteousness.**

   Now to the one who works, wages are not credited as a gift but as an obligation. However, to the one who does not work but trusts God who justifies the ungodly, their faith is credited as righteousness. (Romans 4:4-5)

Earlier in the book of Ephesians, Paul tells the church to abandon their old way of life and embrace the new life that God created for them, with an emphasis on letting the Holy Spirit renew their thoughts and attitudes (Ephesians 4:22-24).

6. **Read the verses below and underline anything that is a gateway to our hearts.**

   I will set no base or wicked thing before my eyes. I hate the work of them who turn aside [from the right path]; it shall not grasp hold of me. (Psalm 101:3, AMP)

   The heart of the discerning acquires knowledge, for the ears of the wise seek it out. (Proverbs 18:15)

   Therefore, "Come out from them and be separate, says the Lord. Touch no unclean thing, and I will receive you." (2 Corinthians 6:17)

Our physical senses are gateways to our hearts. Guarding these gateways helps us set aside the habits and activities that were part of our old nature.

7. **In what practical ways can we guard these gateways to our hearts?**

   _____
   _____
   _____
   _____
   _____

When we receive Jesus Christ as Savior, the Holy Spirit creates new life in us. When we embrace our new nature, we experience the protection that comes from right living.

We aren't perfect and will continue to sin. When we do, however, we confess our sin, knowing that God is faithful to His promise to cleanse us and make us righteous (1 John 1:9). He doesn't see our sin anymore. Instead, He sees the righteousness of His Son.

8. Write a prayer responding to what you've learned today.

Going Deeper: Use BibleGateway to search for the word guard *in your preferred translation. Use the filters on the right to narrow your results to the Book of Proverbs. Take note of who is guarding, what is being guarded, and the results of guarding. Make a summary statement.*

day 3

our enemy exploits our weaknesses

Did God really say…? (Genesis 3:1)

From the beginning of time, Satan's goal has been to separate us from a relationship with God. He knows our weaknesses well and exploits them. He makes sin look enticing, or good, even. All Christians have weaknesses. Regardless of how long we've known the Lord or how far along we are in our walk of faith, we are always vulnerable to temptation.

1. **Read Genesis 2:9-17 and Genesis 3:1-4 and describe how Satan appealed to Eve.**

_____
_____
_____
_____

The first thing Satan did was to question what God said. "Did God really say…" is one of Satan's favorite questions. When he asks this question, he's doing two things. First, he minimizes sin. He says, "It's not *that bad*!" Then he minimizes the consequences of sin. He says, "You're not really going *to die*!" Has Satan ever used this line with you? He has with me, many times.

#standingfirmbiblestudy |109

week 5 | standing firm in Christ

2. How does recognizing this lie help you when you face temptation?

_____
_____
_____

3. Read Luke 18:9-14. In this parable, how did Satan appeal to his mark?

_____
_____
_____

4. What are some everyday examples of self-righteousness?

_____
_____
_____

5. According to Colossians 3:22-23, how does Satan tempt people to sin when they are doing good things?

_____
_____
_____

Perfectionism and trying to please others is exhausting. Sometimes the overwhelm leads us to think living a righteous life is impossible. So why bother? If we find ourselves with this mindset, our eyes are in the wrong place. We are focusing on the *effort* of doing right, rather than the joy of serving God by serving others.

Satan uses any means possible to lead us into sin. He tempts us according to our passions and when we are physically, mentally, or emotionally weak. He will tempt us when we are strong. Satan misuses God's Word and convinces us that our self-righteousness is sufficient. He minimizes sin and its consequences. Satan wants us focused on the effort of doing good things, rather than the joy of serving Christ. He exhausts us when we try to please others, tackle issues, or handle day-to-day concerns in our own strength. Even a "spiritual high" can be a dangerous place for temptation.

6. In what other ways have you found Satan successful at exploiting your weaknesses?

_____
_____
_____
_____
_____

Wearing the Breastplate of Righteousness doesn't mean Satan will leave us alone. He is persistent and skilled at exploiting our weaknesses. Guarding our hearts and shoring up our weaknesses with the truth of God's Word helps us be better prepared when our enemy attacks us.

day 4

standing firm in Christ's righteousness

For those God foreknew he also predestined to be conformed to the image of his Son, that he might be the firstborn among many brothers and sisters. (ROMANS 8:29)

God's foremost purpose for us is to become like Christ. Salvation grants us "positional" righteousness. In other words, we are "in Christ." We are "connected" to Him. When God looks at us, He doesn't see our sin, because Jesus paid our penalty with His blood. God completely forgives us.

But we are human and not perfect. We won't be perfect until we reach our heavenly home. Until then, God works in our lives. As we cooperate with Him, our lives reflect the character of Christ (2 Corinthians 3:18). It's not a life of legalism. Rather, it is a life of love. We obey God out of a heart of love. Sometimes obedience is difficult. Certain life circumstances are beyond our ability to walk through on our own. We need the supernatural enabling that God gives.

This is what happens when we put on the Breastplate of Righteousness. We put on the righteous character of Christ.

1. **Read Colossians 3:5-15. In the table on the next page, in the first column, list the things Paul says to "put off" or "put to death." In the other, list the qualities we are to "put on" or "clothe" ourselves with.**

Put Off / Put to Death	Put On / Clothe

These characteristics grow in our lives as we mature in Christ. As we align our hearts with God's heart, we want to do the things He wants us to do.

Throughout my kids' growing-up years, we told them to choose their friends carefully. We knew they would adopt the habits and thought patterns of those they spent significant time with. Although the negative aspect of this is clearly stated in Scripture (1 Corinthians 15:33), the opposite is also true. And it carries over into our relationship with God. The more time we spend with Him in His Word and in prayer, the more our habits and our thoughts align with His. That is the primary way we grow in godly character.

2. **Read the Scriptures below, and underline other ways God develops and refines our faith.**

> *Consider it pure joy, my brothers and sisters, whenever you face trials of many kinds, because you know that the testing of your faith produces perseverance. Let perseverance finish its work so that you may be mature and complete, not lacking anything.*
> (James 1:2-4)

All Scripture is God-breathed and is useful for teaching, rebuking, correcting and training in righteousness, so that the servant of God may be thoroughly equipped for every good work. (2 Timothy 3:16-17)

In all this you greatly rejoice, though now for a little while you may have had to suffer grief in all kinds of trials. These have come so that the proven genuineness of your faith–of greater worth than gold, which perishes even though refined by fire–may result in praise, glory and honor when Jesus Christ is revealed. (1 Peter 1:6-7)

When God's Word corrects us, we have a decision to make. Will we do our own thing? Or will we yield our will to God's? Go back to Day 1 of this week and read the section on THE SPIRIT OF RIGHTEOUSNESS. Yielding our wills to God is not just a New Testament command. When the Israelites had possessed the Promised Land, Joshua gave them specific instructions.

"Now then" said Joshua, "throw away the foreign gods that are among you and yield your hearts to the LORD, the God of Israel." (Joshua 24:23)

Anything that keeps us from yielding fully to the Lord is an idol and must be removed from our lives.

3. **Write out Ephesians 5:18. Then explain what it means to be "filled with the Spirit."**

_____
_____
_____
_____
_____
_____
_____
_____
_____

Remember that being filled with the Spirit is about who (or what) controls our lives. We get

week 5 | standing firm in Christ

to choose. Each of us has specific weaknesses, areas where we are more vulnerable than others. We must be especially careful with these and guard our hearts and our minds so they don't lead us astray. For example, if spending time with certain friends creates strong temptation, we limit (or eliminate) our time with them.

4. **1 Corinthians 1:30 tells us that God put us "in Christ Jesus." What else does this verse tell us about who we are in Christ?**

_____

_____

_____

There is nothing we can do to earn righteousness. Our salvation, any spiritual knowledge we have, any righteousness displayed in our lives, results from God's work in our lives. Yes, we obey; we submit. But it's not about doing; it's about loving. It's about aligning our hearts with God's heart. It's then that following His commands becomes a joy, not a burden.

day 5

God is completely righteous. Our efforts to be righteous are like filthy rags. Jesus became sin (or unrighteousness) for us, so we could wear His righteousness as a breastplate to protect our hearts, which determines the direction of our lives.

personal action plan

In your spiritual battle, is there an area of your life where you struggle with obedience? Why do you think this is? (Remember what we learned about our hearts!)

_____
_____
_____
_____
_____
_____
_____

Consider what you wrote on Day 1. Since we looked at our hearts this week, do you need to change what you believe and feel about people or things associated with your spiritual battle?

_____
_____
_____
_____
_____
_____

#standingfirmbiblestudy

week 5 | standing firm in Christ

Write out Scriptures that help you yield fully to the Holy Spirit.

Using this Scripture, write a battlefield prayer of commitment.

Find three songs that encourage you to yield fully to the Lord.

week six – the gospel of peace

day 1 – the God of peace

day 2 – the firm foundation of the gospel of peace

day 3 – the enemy of the gospel of peace

day 4 – standing firm with the Prince of Peace

day 5 – personal action plan

week 6 | standing firm in Christ

weekly prep

Welcome to week six where we learn about the gospel of peace! Let's prepare, first! Consider one of your spiritual battles. Has your battle caused a disruption in your personal peace, peace between you and God, or peace between you and someone else? Is there someone in your life who needs to hear the gospel message? Think about how his or her life would be changed by a relationship with Jesus Christ. Take some time to journal what's on your heart about these questions.

_____
_____
_____
_____
_____
_____
_____
_____
_____
_____
_____
_____
_____
_____
_____
_____
_____

day 1

the God of peace

Now may the Lord of peace himself give you peace at all times and in every way. The Lord be with all of you. (2 THESSALONIANS 3:16)

October was always a crazy month for my family. When my kids were younger, it was competition season for my son's karate classes. We usually scheduled a camping trip afterward so we could be together as a family and decompress after a full schedule. Sitting by the fire, reading a book, and going for nature walks worked wonders to prepare us for the end-of-semester push that awaited our return.

During our kids' high school years, we packed October weekends with Friday night lights and all-day Saturday marching band contests. Toss in a couple of out-of-town competitions, and *we were busy*! (Don't even get me started on the extra rehearsals, homework that needed to be completed, and more than a few hours for their jobs.) As a fully involved parent, I attended every performance, served on the Band Booster Board, and was one of the color guard "moms-on-the-spot." I loved every minute. But October made my head spin. There was practically no time for anything other than performances and competitions.

In early November, I attended a beach scrapbooking retreat. As competition season wound down, my desire to escape to the beach increased. I just wanted to get away from the craziness–to a place of quiet and stillness. A place where my body and my soul could be still. I prayed for good weather so I could wake up early and watch the sun rise over the water. Each morning, I sat in my chair with my cup of coffee and waited in the silence. The waves rolled to shore, leaving clumps of foam on the wet sand. Seagulls waded in the shallow surf, hoping to find a tasty bite for breakfast. As night gave way to light, pelicans flew in formation across the ocean expanse, occasionally diving for their meal. Eventually, the sun rose from the horizon, casting hues of pink and orange across the sky, which was reflected in the wet sand. God spoke to my exhausted soul with gorgeous displays of beauty.

Sometimes our souls crave this respite of peace not only because we're overwhelmed from busyness, but because—you know, life. A loved one ends up in ICU. We receive a devastating diagnosis. Job loss. Death of a dear friend or family member. Betrayal from someone we trusted. If life has left you broken and overwhelmed, you know what caused the emptiness.

And while we crave this peace, sometimes retreating to a "peaceful location" is not possible. The good news is God offers His peace right where we are. We don't have to "get away" to experience it.

He Himself is our peace.

GOD IS PEACE

Before the Israelites possessed the Promised Land, God renewed His covenant with them. He promised to bless them if they obeyed Him. But He also promised curses if they were disobedient. The Book of Judges tells the early history of the nation of Israel after they took possession of the Promised Land. Canaan was now their home. For a while they lived at peace in this new land, but eventually, like we do sometimes, they forgot the Lord. They followed God for a while, but when things got comfortable, they started doing things their own way. As a result, God sent other nations to oppress them until they were ready to follow Him again. At that point, God sent a judge, or a leader in Israel, to lead them out of oppression and into freedom.

> We crave peace. Sometimes retreating to a peaceful location is not possible, but God offers His peace right where we are. We don't have to "get away" to experience it. He Himself is our peace.

Judges 6 tells the story of Gideon. Israel had been under the oppression of the Midianites for seven years. Their armies camped nearby and at every opportunity destroyed the crops and ravaged the land of Israel. The Bible says they "swarmed like locusts" on the land, consumed all their crops, and stole their livestock, leaving Israel on the brink of starvation.

One harvest season, instead of threshing wheat in the open where the wind could blow away the chaff (and where he'd be seen by the Midianites), Gideon threshed wheat in a winepress, which was a deep trough. He may have been successful at hiding from the Midianites, but without the wind to blow away the chaff, he was not very effective at threshing his wheat.

In this hidden spot, the angel of the Lord appeared to Gideon and gave him the command to lead the fight against Israel's oppressors. Gideon knew he was speaking with a *representative* from God. He responded by preparing an offering and bringing it to the messenger. The angel of the Lord touched the offering with the tip of his staff and flame immediately consumed the offering. Then Gideon realized he was in the *presence* of God Himself. He was terrified because he knew that no one could see God and live.

But the Lord told him, "Peace! Do not be afraid. You are not going to die" (Judges 6:23). In response, Gideon built an altar to God and named it:

yahweh shalom: THE LORD IS PEACE

Within a moment, Gideon went from panicked to peaceful–all because of God's presence and His promise (Judges 6:23-24).

JESUS–THE PRINCE OF PEACE

Through the prophet Isaiah, God promised to send a Messiah who would bring lasting peace to Israel.

> *For a child is born to us, a son is given to us. The government will rest on his shoulders. And he will be called: Wonderful Counselor, Mighty God, Everlasting Father, Prince of Peace. His government and its peace will never end.* (Isaiah 9:6-7a)

The Messiah's government will have peace that never ends. Can you imagine how the Israelites felt when they heard this? Israel had very few consecutive years of peace with its kings. Occasionally a righteous king, one who followed the Lord, would take the throne. As he led the people to follow the Lord, the nation of Israel experienced a period of peace, with rest from their enemies. For most of their history, Israel's kings led them to follow foreign gods. They were at war much of the time and were eventually taken captive by oppressing nations. To hear that a King was coming who would save them from political unrest must have been music to their ears.

Hundreds of years later, God spoke to a priest named Zechariah. While Zechariah served in the temple, God told him that his barren wife would have a son–who would be the forerunner of the

Messiah. Shortly after John the Baptist's birth, Zechariah prophesied over him and the soon-to-be-born Jesus. He proclaimed that the Messiah would lead them out of darkness into light and that He would guide them in the path of peace (Luke 1:79).

Hallelujah!

A few months later, an angel appeared to some shepherds who were watching over their flocks. He announced the birth of their long-awaited Messiah and left them with the reminder that God would bring peace to those who would repent and follow Christ (Luke 2:14).

When Jesus was born, Israel was no longer an independent nation. The Israelites still lived in the land, but they were governed and oppressed by the Romans.

The Messiah, the promised Prince of Peace, had been born.

The climax of Jesus's ministry was His triumphal entry into Jerusalem. On the Sunday before Passover, Jesus sent two of His disciples to bring Him a young colt. It was customary for a new king to ride into his conquered city so the people would recognize him as their ruler.

But Jesus did this differently; He rode a small donkey. No pomp and circumstance. But the message was the same. Somewhere between Bethany and Jerusalem, a crowd of disciples spread their cloaks on the ground and praised God for all the miracles Jesus had done. In their excitement they shouted:

> *Blessings on the King who comes in the name of the LORD! Peace in heaven, and glory in highest heaven!* (Luke 19:38)

At His birth, the angels proclaimed, "peace on earth," (Luke 2:14). Interestingly, now the crowd proclaimed, "peace in heaven." They did not have a full understanding of who Jesus was. Little did they know at what cost this peace–and their peace–would come.

Truly, God brought His peace from heaven to earth in His Son.

Until this time, Jesus had not sought to be called the Messiah. But now He allowed it and even encouraged it. Everything He did the week before His crucifixion was designed to call attention to the fact that He was the Messiah.[11]

At the end of the week, Jesus shared the Passover meal with His disciples. He washed their feet, encouraged them, and prayed for them. They didn't understand everything He said and did. But Jesus promised that eventually they would (John 13:7).

the God of peace | day 1

Although Jesus came to bring peace, His ministry was fraught with antagonism. He told His disciples (and us) to expect ridicule and persecution because they stood for Him. Life would not be easy, but difficult. They would face trials, sorrow, and persecution, but they didn't need to worry or be afraid. He had overcome the world (John 16:33). He said:

> *Peace I leave with you; My [perfect] peace I give to you; not as the world gives do I give to you. Do not let your heart be troubled, nor let it be afraid. [Let My perfect peace calm you in every circumstance and give you courage and strength for every challenge.]*
> (John 14:27, AMP)

When our world (within and without) is in upheaval, we cannot survive without some semblance of peace to keep us steady. The peace Jesus gives is more than a parting gift. It is essential for our survival.

FRUIT OF THE SPIRIT

When Franklin Planners® first came out, I thought I was in heaven. Then it was my Palm Pilot® and next my Dell® Axim. Everything I needed was at my fingertips without my having to lug around five pounds of leather and paper. With these organizational tools, I thought I could live in real peace. I was in control of my environment. What I didn't know was, with this perceived level of control, I got involved in more and more activities.

Our culture is blessed with advanced technology that is supposed to improve our lives, but sometimes it leads us to become overly busy with heads spinning. I am an organized person, but I don't *enjoy* organizing. I love the result! Which, if I'm honest, is control. When I am in control, I am at peace. When I know where things are, I'm not frustrated trying to find them. And *if* something is misplaced, oh, the anxiety of trying to find it.

True peace is not being organized. It's not even about being a "minimalist." Although spinning fewer plates and caring for less "stuff" certainly frees up more than a few brain cells, true peace is being settled with our God–focusing on Him, not on our circumstances.

When we let the Holy Spirit control our minds, we experience life and peace (Romans 8:5-6). When we move our focus away from the Lord, we allow our circumstances and our cravings to dominate us, and this produces frustration, anxiety, and disappointment. Our focus has everything to do with how we live within our circumstances and how we come out of them.

God's Promise of Peace

The Book of Habakkuk, one of the shortest books in the Old Testament, is a discussion between him and God about the current state of affairs, in Israel. *The Bible Knowledge Commentary* says, "Unlike other prophets who declared God's message to people, this prophet dialogued with God about people."[12]

Habakkuk was frustrated about the violence and injustice around him. He didn't understand God's plan to punish Israel by allowing them to be captured by an evil nation. God was not offended with his questions; in fact, He answered them. Habakkuk continued questioning God and God graciously answered. By the end of the book, Habakkuk's resolve was firm.

What began with a question mark ended in an exclamation point. The answer to Habakkuk's "Why?" was "Who!" His confusion, "Why all the conflict?" was resolved with his comprehension of who was in control: God![13] He ends his book with this song of praise and trust:

> *Even though the fig trees have no blossoms, and there are no grapes on the vines; even though the olive crop fails, and the fields lie empty and barren; even though the flocks die in the fields, and the cattle barns are empty, yet I will rejoice in the LORD! I will be joyful in the God of my salvation! The Sovereign LORD is my strength! He makes me as surefooted as a deer, able to tread upon the heights.* (Habakkuk 3:17-19)

The same can be said for us. We live in a world filled with sin. We see it in our news outlets, our high schools, our families, and in our hospitals. When we focus on our circumstances, anxiety threatens to rule. But when we focus on God, His peace reigns within our hearts.

Israel was unfaithful to God throughout her history. He punished her for her unfaithfulness but always promised that peace would come. God fulfilled His promise when He sent the Prince of Peace in His Son, Jesus Christ.

> *"Though the mountains be shaken and the hills be removed, yet my unfailing love for you will not be shaken nor my covenant of peace be removed," says the LORD, who has compassion on you.* (Isaiah 54:10)

day 2

the firm foundation of the gospel of peace

And with your feet fitted with the readiness that comes from the gospel of peace.
(EPHESIANS 6:15)

Shoes are an essential part of any wardrobe. I have a good number of shoes in my closet. My dressy shoes have high heels. My everyday shoes are blinged-out flip-flops. And I have some athletic shoes. I would never wear my flip-flops to the gym. They aren't designed for that. They are for running around town and having lunch with my girlfriends.

By the same token, I would not wear my hiking boots with a dress I wear to a wedding. My athletic shoes are for working out. My plain flip-flops are for the beach. (Yes, even flip-flops are designed for different activities!) And my slippers are for lazy mornings at home. Each pair of shoes is designed for a specific purpose.

The same was true for a Roman soldier's shoes. They were made with cleats on the bottom so the soldier could stand firm in battle.[14] On slippery ground, they provided extra traction so he wouldn't fall.

For believers, our battle shoes must do the same. Not just any shoe will do. Paul told the Ephesians to have their feet "fitted with readiness." The Greek word for "readiness" is **hetoimasía**, which means "preparation or a basis, a firm foundation or firm footing."[15]

Our battle shoes are a solid understanding of the good news that makes us prepared to defend and share the gospel of peace with a world that is lost and desperately seeking it.

1. **Write out Isaiah 52:7 and emphasize what makes the feet of these messengers beautiful.**

   _____
   _____
   _____
   _____

   This Scripture carries implications for the time it was written as well as for the future. After oppression and subjugation by the Babylonians, the Israelites were free to return to their homes. The feet of the messenger who carried this news were, indeed, beautiful. This future messenger carries the good news that their promised Messiah will reign in Zion. There will be no more war. Instead of hostility, peace! Instead of slavery, salvation! What hope this must have brought them.

   It brings hope for us, too. One day, we will no longer live in a world filled with conflict and oppression. King Jesus will reign and bring His peace! For today, amid our deepest struggles, His peace reigns in our hearts.

2. **Read Luke 2:8-11, and describe the "good news."**

   _____
   _____

   The word *gospel* means "good news." Jesus offered His perfect life as the perfect sacrifice for our sin. We've learned that our righteousness does not meet God's requirement for the penalty of sin. But Jesus's perfect life and death does. This is the heart of the gospel of peace. That Jesus would willingly give His life for us is good news!

3. **According to 2 Corinthians 5:17-20, with what have we been entrusted?**

   _____
   _____
   _____
   _____

the firm foundation of the gospel of peace | day 2

Through faith in Christ, we have peace with God (Romans 5:1). As a result, we are given the ministry and message of reconciliation. Once we have been reconciled to God, we carry the gospel message to others so they, too, can be reconciled to Him.

4. **Read 1 Corinthians 15:1-6 below and underline the elements that make up the gospel.**

   Now, brothers and sisters, I want to remind you of the gospel I preached to you, which you received and on which you have taken your stand. By this gospel you are saved, if you hold firmly to the word I preached to you. Otherwise, you have believed in vain. For what I received I passed on to you as of first importance: that Christ died for our sins according to the Scriptures, that he was buried, that he was raised on the third day according to the Scriptures, and that he appeared to Cephas, and then to the Twelve. After that, he appeared to more than five hundred of the brothers and sisters at the same time, most of whom are still living, though some have fallen asleep. (1 Corinthians 15:1-6)

   When we know the elements that make up the gospel, we can share it with others!

   - Christ died for our sins.
   - He was buried.
   - He was raised on the third day.
   - He appeared to Peter, the disciples, and more than five hundred others.

5. **List friends or family who need to hear the gospel of peace. What impact would their hearing the gospel of peace have in their lives?**

   _____
   _____
   _____
   _____
   _____
   _____
   _____

#standingfirmbiblestudy

day 3

the enemy of the gospel of peace

The thief comes only to steal and kill and destroy. I have come that they may have life, and have it to the full. (JOHN 10:10)

Yesterday we learned that we have been entrusted with the message and ministry of reconciliation: sharing the gospel of peace with a world that is desperately seeking it. Leading others to salvation is the greatest peacemaking privilege given to us. We get to show people how they can have peace with God, know peace amid their trials, and spend eternity with Him. Satan wants the opposite. He will interfere by interrupting our circumstances, by causing us to fear the outcome of sharing our message of faith, or by creating confusion or distraction in the heart and mind of the one listening.

Have you ever been in a conversation with someone and were prompted to steer the topic toward spiritual things, in hopes a door would open for you to share the gospel? Just when you're ready to ask a key question, something happens. The doorbell rings. They get a phone call. Someone else walks up and joins your conversation.

Maybe you simply don't know what to say or how to start a spiritually focused conversation, or you had a perfect opportunity to talk about Jesus, but you became paralyzed with fear. Perhaps you were afraid your friend would reject you, that you wouldn't be able to communicate effectively, or that you wouldn't be able to answer their questions. You might have even felt that once word was out that you were "that kind of Christian" (one bold enough to share your faith), you would be judged or labeled a hypocrite. This fear is normal and a tool the enemy uses to keep us from being effective.

There may have been times when you did everything right. You prayed, and God opened a door. You shared, but your friend rejected the message. All these experiences may lead us to believe that *we* are not ones who can share the gospel and lead people to salvation. So why bother? This response is exactly what Satan hopes for. He wants fear to silence us and frustration to immobilize us.

We must fight that! God has called us to the important work of sharing the gospel! Satan would like nothing more than to keep us from this mission. God wants to give us life. Satan wants to destroy life.

As we dig into this day's study, please don't start with one ounce of fear or self-condemnation. God has a plan for *you* to share His message of peace. At the end of today, I'll share some resources and encouragement I've found helpful.

1. **Have you ever shared (or tried to share) the gospel with someone? Have you ever felt led to share but decided not to? What kept you from doing so?**

___
___
___
___
___
___
___

When we begin a relationship with God, we are no longer under His wrath. Peace is established between us and Him. As a result, we can experience His day-to-day peace in the middle of painful circumstances. But Satan will continue to disrupt our lives and try to destroy that peace.

the enemy of the gospel of peace | day 3

2. **Read the passages below and underline the enemies of peace Satan uses.**

   They are conceited and understand nothing. They have an unhealthy interest in controversies and quarrels about words that result in envy, strife, malicious talk, evil suspicions and constant friction between people of corrupt mind, who have been robbed of the truth and who think that godliness is a means to financial gain. (1 Timothy 6:4-5)

   Therefore I tell you, do not worry about your life, what you will eat or drink; or about your body, what you will wear. Is not life more than food, and the body more than clothes? Look at the birds of the air; they do not sow or reap or store away in barns, and yet your heavenly Father feeds them. Are you not much more valuable than they? Can any one of you by worrying add a single hour to your life? (Matthew 6:25-27)

3. **Look up the following verses and identify more enemies of peace.**

Psalm 31:9	
Ephesians 4:31	
Philippians 4:6-7	
Philippians 4:11-12	
James 3:16	

Satan will stop at nothing to keep us from being effective for the Lord. He will do whatever he can to keep unbelievers from finding Christ. For some, he may try to keep life comfortable and unchallenging, to the extent they don't recognize their need for salvation. Others he will lead to utter destruction.

He does the same to believers. We are not exempt from his schemes. Even our children are not off-limits to him. He may create situations with their friends that cause them deep grief, which in turn causes parents turmoil. He uses extramarital sex, drugs, alcohol–anything to drive us into anxiety. Remember, Satan is a schemer. Paul told the Ephesians:

#standingfirmbiblestudy

> *Put on the full armor of God, so that you can take your stand against the devil's schemes.* (Ephesians 6:11)

The Greek word for schemes is ***methodeia***, and it means (you guessed it) method[16]. A method is a specific plan. Satan doesn't go after us willy-nilly. He knows us well and devises specific plans to derail us. He creates circumstances that can cause us to spin off in anxiety. Often, we don't realize what's going on until we are in the middle of it. So, when you find yourself at odds with yourself (and others), remember that the enemy of your soul has you right where he wants you. It's then that you get to choose how you will respond.

4. Are you aware of the schemes Satan uses most effectively against you? What can you do about it?

_____
_____
_____
_____
_____

WHEN YOU WANT TO SHARE THE GOSPEL OF PEACE

I am not an expert in evangelism, but I have learned a few things that help me be confident in sharing the gospel.

- If someone rejects the gospel message, they are rejecting Jesus, not the messenger. It may feel like they are rejecting us, but they aren't.

- Our carefully crafted words do not cause someone to choose Christ. The Holy Spirit will give us the right words at the right time when it's time for us to speak (Luke 12:12). Although it can be helpful to have a plan for sharing the gospel, we can stumble and stutter through it. God is bigger and will use our weaknesses to accomplish great things.

- We don't have to share the entire gospel message, only what God leads us to share. Sometimes our job is simply to plant a seed. Paul told the Corinthians that it didn't matter *who* shared the gospel. He planted the seed, Apollos watered it, but God makes the seed grow (1 Corinthians 3:6-7). We don't have to be *the ones* who pray someone through the salvation experience. We just have to be faithful to what God calls us to do.

- Remember what's at stake if we don't share. Yes, it's scary, but people's eternity hangs in the balance. God is with us and strengthens us to speak His gospel of peace.

When I first learned to share the gospel, my coach told me to memorize *The Four Spiritual Laws*[17], a pamphlet published by what was then Campus Crusade for Christ. This was so I didn't have to focus on reading it. If I was sitting across the table from someone, I could have the pamphlet facing them while I shared what was inside. Although I don't use that pamphlet anymore, its content forms the basis for every evangelistic encounter I have. I encourage you to find something you like and learn it well. Below are some resources I've found helpful.

- How to Know God – https://www.cru.org/us/en/how-to-know-god

- Steps to Peace with God – https://stepstopeace.org

- The Wordless Book (for children) – https://www.letthelittlechildrencome.com

day 4

standing firm with the Prince of Peace

Be alert and of sober mind. Your enemy the devil prowls around like a roaring lion looking for someone to devour. Resist him, standing firm in the faith, because you know that the family of believers throughout the world is undergoing the same kind of sufferings.

(1 Peter 5:8-9)

The title Prince of Peace conveys a variety of meanings. The word "prince" carries the idea of royalty, of government, and of rule. Peace is the goal of most nations. No country wants to be at war. War not only puts a significant strain on the economy, it also costs lives, resulting in grief, despondence, and general unrest. National leaders do all they can to maintain peace for their countries. But as Christians, we are in a war we cannot avoid. Our enemy will not be sated. Much of standing firm against our enemy begins with being aware. When we are in circumstances that are anything but peaceful, it helps if we can stop and recognize them for what they are. Although God is not the author of confusion, Any confusing circumstances in our lives, He allows for a specific purpose.

1. **Read James 1:2-4 and 1 Peter 1:6-7. Why may God allow difficult circumstances to enter our lives?**

_____

_____

_____

week 6 | standing firm in Christ

2. According to John 14:27 and John 16:33, what did Jesus say about peace?

_____

_____

_____

No matter how committed to the Lord we may be, difficulties are unavoidable. If we aren't in the middle of one, we probably just came out of one or are headed into another. It's part of life. The troubles we experience may not be ours specifically. They may result from crises involving our children, dear friends, our churches and schools, even our aging parents. We need a strategy for gaining peace when our world is upended.

> *Depression is a serious mental health issue in our world today. Counseling and/or medication are often necessary, sometimes for the short term, sometimes long term. God still wants to work through these difficult circumstances. Let's not miss out on it!*

3. Write out Isaiah 26:3-4, emphasizing what is most important about peace.

_____

_____

_____

_____

Jesus faced agonizing torture when He was crucified for us. Yet He endured. Hebrews 12:1-3 tells us how.

4. Read Hebrews 12:1-3 below and underline what Jesus did to endure His crucifixion.

> *Therefore, since we are surrounded by such a great cloud of witnesses, let us throw off everything that hinders and the sin that so easily entangles. And let us run with perseverance the race marked out for us, fixing our eyes on Jesus, the pioneer and perfecter of faith. For the joy set before him he endured the cross, scorning its shame, and sat down at the right hand of the throne of God. Consider him who endured such opposition from sinners, so that you will not grow weary and lose heart.*
> (Hebrews 12:1-3)

The world numbs the pain of difficult situations with temporal pleasures such as drugs, alcohol, or sex. Some retreat into television or electronic devices, isolating and insulating themselves from the reality of their problems.

As Christians, sometimes we do the same things, but we have a better alternative. Our Savior endured the cross "for the joy set before Him." That joy? It's us! To endure the excruciating pain of the cross, Jesus focused on the joy He would experience with us in eternity.

We can do the same thing. To endure the difficulties of our trials, we focus on Jesus and the joy we will share with Him in eternity! Sometimes our trials *are* more than we can bear. But Jesus meets us where we are. As we focus on Him, He sustains us. The world observes this, and God receives glory.

5. What does a heart at peace look like?

_____

_____

_____

_____

6. What are some ways we can focus on Jesus?

_____

_____

_____

_____

day 5

We wear battle shoes that represent our readiness to share the gospel of peace. This "firm foundation" enables us to experience God's peace in our spiritual battles and share that peace with others.

personal action plan

Jesus Christ is the Prince of Peace, who came to reconcile us with God. His presence brings peace amid our struggles. Where in your life (or with whom) do you need peace?

_____
_____
_____
_____
_____
_____
_____

Ask God to reveal with whom He wants you to share the gospel of peace.

_____
_____
_____
_____
_____
_____
_____

week 6 | standing firm in Christ

Write out Scriptures that help you focus on Jesus and bring peace to your heart.

_____
_____
_____
_____
_____
_____
_____
_____
_____

Using these Scriptures, write a battlefield prayer of commitment.

_____
_____
_____
_____
_____
_____
_____
_____
_____
_____
_____

Find three songs that bring peace to your heart.

_____
_____
_____

week seven – the shield of faith

day 1 – our faithful God

day 2 – the shield of faith

day 3 – our enemy's flaming arrows

day 4 – standing firm in our God's faithfulness

day 5 – personal action plan

weekly prep

What struggles are you facing today? Do you trust God to protect you in your battle? What kind of doubts do you have? Once again, be honest with yourself and God! It makes a difference!!

day 1

our faithful God

Know therefore that the Lord your God is God; he is the faithful God, keeping his covenant of love to a thousand generations of those who love him and keep his commandments.

(DEUTERONOMY 7:9)

This week we will look at two aspects of God's nature: His faithfulness and His protectiveness described as a shield. Taken together, we learn that as we follow God and trust Him fully, He protects us with the very words He speaks. Unless God specifically allows it, nothing can penetrate His shield around us. In Week 4 we looked at the Hebrew word *emet*, which means *truth*. We also learned that, depending on the context, one Hebrew word can be translated into different English words. This is the case in the verses below. Because we worship and serve the one true God, we can trust Him fully as He protects us with the shield of His faithfulness.

> *He will cover you with his feathers, and under his wings you will find refuge; his faithfulness will be your shield and rampart.* (Psalm 91:4)

> *This God–his way is perfect; the word of the Lord proves true; he is a shield for all those who take refuge in him.* (Psalm 18:30, ESV)

OUR FAITHFUL GOD IS OUR SHIELD

In Genesis 12, the Lord called Abram to leave his people and follow Him to a land He would later show him. Abram and his wife Sarai were old and had no children, but the Lord promised him he would become the father of a great nation. They gathered all their belongings, left the land of Ur, and began the journey of following a God they barely knew. Genesis 15 details the covenant God made with Abram, which includes this beautiful promise as its preamble.

Do not be afraid, Abram. I am your shield, your very great reward. (Genesis 15:1)

A shield is a protective barrier that keeps everything on one side from penetrating to the other side, thus protecting the one holding it. God is described as our rock, fortress, deliverer, stronghold– and our shield (Psalm 18:2). When we take refuge in God as our Shield, He protects us (Psalm 18:30).

> *Going Deeper: Go to biblegateway.com and type* God shield *or* Lord shield *(without quotation marks) in the search bar. It will pull up all the verses in the Bible that have those two words in them. You'll see that it's not just in Psalms where we see God as our shield. Type* refuge shield *in the search bar and see what else shows up. Type* you shield *to see where God or Lord was mentioned in the previous verse, but they didn't change the subject. You can filter your list with the options displayed to the right.*

How do we take refuge in God?

Taking refuge in God is connecting with Him whenever we are in need. It might be as simple as talking to Him about our troubles or hurts. Sometimes it is crying out to Him in desperation. No matter what's going on in our lives, God wants us to come to Him. When we draw near to Him, He draws near to us (James 4:8).

Taking refuge in God is also grabbing our Bibles and reading Scripture for as long as it takes for our thoughts and emotions to settle down. We might start reading through Psalms or choose one verse to meditate on, one word at a time. Through this process, the Holy Spirit speaks truth to our hearts, and we experience peace.

> Because we worship and serve the one true God, we can trust Him fully as He protects us with the shield of His faithfulness.

We may take refuge in God through worship. Sometimes I turn the volume up on my playlist, thinking the louder it is, the deeper the truth I'm singing will sink into my head and my heart. Other times I simply need to be in nature. I pack a lunch and go to a state park not too far away where I can be alone with the Lord and enjoy all kinds of wildlife. Walking along the trails I get to see alligators sunning on the edge of the lakes and blue herons standing at attention with their amazing head plumes blowing in the breeze. Green pollen collects on the surface of the small lakes. It's kind of scary for those with serious allergies, but I think it's pretty. You may not have a nature refuge nearby, but even a walk through the neighborhood can be calming. Sitting on the sidewalk and watching an ant cross to the other side can be an act of worship, as well. Each thing God created is stunning in its detail and awe inspiring in its simplicity.

When we spend time with God, He stills our hearts. Sometimes God changes our circumstances. Often, however, He works His peace and strength in us so we can endure our circumstances. If God just zapped our circumstances away, we wouldn't grow in strength and perseverance. It takes the winds of adversity to strengthen us. That's when the watching world sees Him in action through our lives.

GOD IS FAITHFUL

Our covenant God keeps the promises He makes. The Bible is filled with promises God made and kept, many of which are being fulfilled even now. We can count on Him to keep every promise He makes to you and me. God told Noah He was going to destroy the earth with a flood–but He would save Noah's family. It took about one hundred years for Noah to build the Ark, then God did exactly what He said He would do. Noah, his family, and pairs of every animal entered the Ark, and it stormed for forty days and nights–covering the entire earth with water. After the flood waters receded, God gave Noah a rainbow as a sign that He would never destroy the earth by flood again. Even today, after every storm we see God's reminder of this covenant promise (Genesis 6-9).

Isaac was born twenty-five years after the promise God made to Abram. (Genesis 21). God led the Israelites out of Egypt after four hundred years of slavery and oppression (Exodus 12).

God. Is. Faithful.

In Deuteronomy 7:9, we find another beautiful Hebrew name for God. ***El*** is paired with ***aman,*** which means "to be firm, to build up, to support, to nurture, or to establish. Metaphorically, the word conveys the notion of faithfulness and trustworthiness, such that one could fully depend on."[18]

el aman: THE FAITHFUL GOD

God promised the Israelites they would possess Canaan, a land flowing with milk and honey. They wandered for forty years before entering it. By the end of the Book of Joshua, each tribe possessed its portion of the land. God fulfilled every promise He made to them as they took the land.

> *So the Lord gave Israel all the land he had sworn to give their ancestors, and they took possession of it and settled there. The LORD gave them rest on every side, just as he had sworn to their ancestors. Not one of their enemies withstood them; the LORD gave all their enemies into their hands. Not one of all the LORD'S good promises to Israel failed; every one was fulfilled.* (Joshua 21:43-45)

God promised Joseph he would be a respected leader. It took a long time for Joseph to realize that dream, but it came true. God used Joseph to save many nations from starvation with his plan to harvest excess grain and share it in years of famine. He saved his own family, as well (Genesis 37-47).

When we read our Bibles, we often see the words *God will, the Lord will,* or *He will*. Everything God says *He will* do is a promise. The *will nots* are important, as well. So, when you're reading your Bible, look for the *wills* and the *will nots* to see our Faithful God at work!

The greatest example of God's faithfulness was His promise to send the Messiah–His Son, Jesus Christ. It's a promise God first made to Adam & Eve (Genesis 3:15) and continually confirmed throughout the Old Testament.

> *Therefore the Lord himself will give you a sign: The virgin will conceive and give birth to a son, and will call him Immanuel.* (Isaiah 7:14)

Paul told the Corinthians that Jesus was God's "yes" to every promise He made to Israel. He is also God's "yes" to us when we choose Christ as our Savior (2 Corinthians 1:20).

JESUS–FAITHFUL AND TRUE

At God's appointed time, Jesus was born. He lived a perfect life and was faithful to complete the work God sent Him to do, which was sharing the Good News in the regions where He lived (Luke 4:43). The same scenario played out again and again. When Jesus entered a town and began teaching, crowds gathered to listen. Because of His compassion for them, He healed their sick and cast out evil spirits.

While in Capernaum, Jesus stayed at Peter's house, where word spread of all He had done. Mark tells us the entire town showed up at the front door. Jesus healed many people that night. The next morning, He slipped away from the house to be alone with His Father. Peter finally found Him and said, "Everyone is looking for You!" But Jesus told him it was time to go to another town to preach the Good News. Although the people wanted Him to stay, Jesus knew He needed to travel so more people could hear the gospel message, for this was why He came (Mark 1:16-39).

Jesus was human. He experienced physical weakness, vulnerability, and the same temptations we do. He understands what it feels like to be in need and in want–and to be within an inch of having it. But Jesus was faithful. He did not sin–ever.

Jesus did not shrink in fear when Israel's religious leaders questioned Him. Instead, He faced difficulty head on. Jesus faced the worst of humanity. In His moment of deepest need, His closest friends betrayed and abandoned him, leaving Him alone to face a mock trial. He was condemned and crucified for crimes He did not commit. He could have called a thousand angels to rescue Him, but out of His great love for us, He chose not to.

Because He loved us, He set His eyes on what lay ahead (eternity with us) and remained faithful (Hebrews 12:2) to His purpose in coming–our redemption! Paul told Timothy, "If we are unfaithful, he remains faithful, for he cannot deny who he is" (2 Timothy 2:13). Jesus is faithful. It's *who He is*. One day, He will return on a white horse, ready to wage war against our enemy. God reveals His name to us: *Faithful and True!* (Revelation 19:11).

Before Jesus died, He promised His disciples that the Father would send the Holy Spirit to live in us, to seal us, to help us walk the Christian life, and to remind us of the things He taught. Forty days after His ascension, all the believers were together in one place. God was faithful once again. He fulfilled His promise and filled all of them with the Holy Spirit.

THE HOLY SPIRIT IS FAITHFUL TO COMPLETE THE WORK GIVEN TO HIM

Like Christ, the Holy Spirit is faithful to complete the work God assigned Him. The first work the Holy Spirit does for a believer is to give us new life through spiritual birth.

> *But when the kindness and love of God our Savior appeared, he saved us, not because of righteous things we had done, but because of his mercy. He saved us through the washing of rebirth and renewal by the Holy Spirit.* (Titus 3:4-5)

The Holy Spirit Seals Our Salvation for Eternity with God

When one of my daughters was searching for an apartment at college, we talked about deposits and how they "guarantee" your place. With thousands of college students vying for prime real estate, that deposit was important. She and her roommates needed assurance that when it came time to move, they had a place to go. And not just *any* place, but a place that fit their needs.

When we are saved, God places the Holy Spirit in our hearts as a seal of ownership. In this way, the Holy Spirit acts as a deposit, guaranteeing our "place" with Him in eternity (2 Corinthians 1:11-12). Jesus told His disciples that when He left them, He would prepare a home for them. That's for us, too. A home designed just for us, suited to our needs there.

GOD IS UNCHANGING

When you were a child, did you ever play with your shadow? Depending on how the sun is shining, your shadow is long or short. Sometimes there are two shadows. They change all the time. They are never an accurate representation of who we are. James tells us that God, who created the sun, the moon, and the stars, does not change like shifting shadows (James 1:17). He created the lights that cause shadows, but He doesn't change like shadows do.

God never changes. He doesn't change His mind like we do (Numbers 23:19). Jesus is unchanging. The writer of Hebrews tells us that Jesus is the same yesterday, today, and forever (Hebrews 13:8). Even when we hurt Him, He doesn't withhold His love. His moods don't change on a whim. It doesn't matter how bad our day is or how big our mistakes are; He is unwavering.

When I was in college, I measured my relationship with God by my circumstances. If I didn't make a good grade on a test, I was certain it was because I didn't have a quiet time that morning. (Nevermind that I hadn't studied well the night before!) If there was a problem in a relationship with one of my roommates, I knew it was because I hadn't spent enough time in God's Word that day. Even now, I sometimes feel like my bad days result from rushing through or not having a quiet time.

But God is not like that. He doesn't love us more because we have a quiet time. He doesn't love us any less because we don't. His love is constant.

God Keeps Every Promise He Makes

God promised the Messiah. He fulfilled that promise when He sent His Son, Jesus, to live among us. He lived a perfect life but died a criminal's death on our behalf. He rose from the grave, conquering sin and death.

Jesus promised the Holy Spirit. God fulfilled that promise when He sent the Holy Spirit at Pentecost. The Holy Spirit now indwells us at the moment of salvation, enabling us to obey God and to live a victorious Christian life. When we leave this earth, God assures us of a sinless, glorious eternity with Him.

Our God is completely faithful. He began working in our lives before we were ever born. From the moment of our birth, He has been working to bring us into a relationship with Him. And it doesn't stop when we are saved. Because He loves us so much, He continues working so we become more and more like His Son (Philippians 1:6).

How have you taken refuge in God and experienced Him as your shield?
_____
_____
_____
_____
_____
_____
_____
_____
_____
_____
_____
_____
_____
_____
_____
_____

> ***Going Deeper:*** *Using the NLT (New Living Translation), do another BibleGateway search for* spirit guarantee *(no quotation marks). You can use other translations, but you'll miss some. The NIV refers to the Holy Spirit with the pronoun* who.
>
> *Do another BibleGateway search looking for* deposit guarantee *(no quotation marks). Filter the New Testament verses.*

day 2

the shield of faith

In addition to all this, take up the shield of faith, with which you can extinguish all the flaming arrows of the evil one. (EPHESIANS 6:16)

What is a shield? We see shields in many "champion dramas." Captain America and Wonder Woman have their shields. Violet Incredible creates a bubble force field around herself. Similarly, the Starship Enterprise has its own protective shield. Nothing penetrates a shield. Everything inside is safe from enemy attack.

When Paul told the Ephesians to take up the Shield of Faith, he was describing the shield carried by Roman soldiers. Captain America's shield is about two to two-and-a-half feet in diameter. A rather small but powerful shield for our superhero. In comparison, a Roman soldier's shield was huge! Approximately two by four feet, it was made of wood and covered with leather that the soldiers kept oiled. When he held it in front of him, it protected the soldier from flaming arrows, a common weapon in that day.[19]

SAVING FAITH

We experience saving faith, faith that leads to eternal salvation, when we put our faith and trust in Jesus Christ's death as payment for our sin. Our culture focuses on achievement, approval, and hard work, but no effort on our part will save us from eternal separation from God (Ephesians 2:8-9). We can't do enough good things or like enough unlikable people. Our salvation is a gift from God that we cannot earn.

#standingfirmbiblestudy |153

week 7 | standing firm in Christ

1. **Describe your salvation story. You don't have to write a lot. The following questions will help you narrow your focus.**

   What was your life like before you came to Christ? What was the catalyst that made you realize you needed Him? How is your life different now that you know Christ?

the shield of faith | day 2

GROWING FAITH

A shield protects us in battle, and battle is where our faith grows. Sometimes, though, it feels like we've been thrown into a battle that is tougher than our ability to stand firm. That's okay!

2. According to Romans 5:3-4, how does our faith grow?

___

3. How have you seen your own faith grow according to the above pattern?

___

4. According to Romans 8:31 and 37, why can we have victory in battles bigger than we are?

___

Testing is how everything grows. It just looks different in different circumstances. If you plant a tree in your yard, you might support it with stakes and rope for a brief time until it's firmly rooted in the ground. But soon you remove the support so it can develop strength as winds blow. If you enjoy athletics, you know that building muscle and endurance requires pushing your body beyond its current abilities.

It's the same with our faith. We read God's Word, and we learn about His character, and how He wants our faith to grow. We read stories about how other people were challenged and how their

week 7 | standing firm in Christ

faith grew. But that's just knowledge. Just like the athlete's, our faith muscles don't grow until we have our own challenging experiences. It's where we exercise what we've learned and push our faith beyond its current state.

5. **When have you recognized the enemy trying to cause you to abandon your faith and your trust in God?**

_____
_____
_____
_____
_____

6. **What can you do to counter this type of attack in the future?**

_____
_____
_____
_____
_____

Even though our tests, challenges, or suffering are more than we can bear, God is with us. He will walk us through them. We may feel beat up by the time we come through a challenge–even physically and emotionally depleted. But our faith will be stronger.

You may know someone who has powerful faith and think, "There's no way I could be as strong as my friend." But that's not true. God loves you. He created you and is committed to growing powerful faith in your life! (Philippians 1:6)

Our unwavering faith in God, coupled with understanding how to use the Sword of the Spirit, helps us defeat our enemy. He is clever, but God is greater!

> *You, dear children, are from God and have overcome them, because the one who is in you is greater than the one who is in the world.* (1 John 4:4)

day 3

our enemy's flaming arrows

In addition to all this, take up the shield of faith, with which you can extinguish all the flaming arrows of the evil one. (EPHESIANS 6:16)

While the armor that directly touched the Roman soldier's body provided up-close protection, his shield supplied another layer of protection. With the shield in place, the soldier could ward off fiery arrows from reaching his body armor. Satan's fiery arrows are anything he sends your way to throw you off balance–or to waylay you completely. Satan wants to undermine our *faith*.

What is the opposite of faith? Doubt!

Satan's goal is to make us doubt God's Word, His ways, and His love for us. Remember that our enemy is a liar and the father of lies (John 8:44). The flaming arrows of lies were his first method of attack with Eve (Genesis 3:1-7).

1. **Read Ephesians 4:26-27. What other kinds of arrows does Satan lob our way?**

___

___

___

Satan wants us to believe lies about everything! About God, about ourselves, about our relationships with others. He wants to keep us angry with people different from us and with those who have hurt us. If we aren't angry with someone, Satan often tries to make us think we aren't whole or complete without certain relationships, or a specific someone, in our lives. Our desires are born of lies that tell us we need or deserve to have something.

2. Read James 1:13-15, and describe the pathway to sin.

_____

_____

_____

_____

Sometimes Satan plants desires in our hearts, but often sin begins with our own desires. The more we think about something, the more enticing the sin becomes. Finally, if we allow it, desire gives birth to sin, and sin gives birth to death (Romans 6:23). It doesn't have to be that way, though.

3. Write out 1 Corinthians 10:13, and emphasize God's provision for temptation.

_____

_____

_____

_____

To overcome temptation, we must build the habit of *looking* for a way out. This is our opportunity to pause what we're doing, look for a way out, and stand firm in the truth that we know.

Satan raises doubts, but Jesus says, "Only believe!"

Throughout His ministry, Jesus healed many people. On one occasion, a crowd had pressed in against Him. A synagogue leader made His way to Jesus and asked Him to heal his dying daughter. At the same time, a woman who had been bleeding for twelve years also struggled to reach Jesus. When she got within an arm's reach of Him, she touched His cloak and her bleeding stopped immediately! Jesus sensed that power had gone out of Him and asked who touched Him. She fell at His feet and admitted it was her. Jesus's response is one of tenderness.

> *Daughter, your faith has healed you. Go in peace and be freed from your suffering.*
> (Mark 5:34)

By the time Jesus could speak with the synagogue leader, his little girl had died. Someone from his home told him not to bother Jesus anymore. But Jesus overheard. Again, His words were full of compassion.

Don't be afraid; just believe. (Mark 5:36)

Jesus followed the man home and healed his daughter. Jesus told both people to believe. To have faith! Faith was His answer to their need. It's His answer to our needs, as well. After Jesus rose from the dead, He appeared to many of His disciples, but He hadn't seen Thomas yet. Thomas doubted. He was adamant that he would not believe until he had proof. Jesus wasn't difficult with Thomas. As usual, He was full of compassion.

4. Read John 20:24-29. How did Jesus meet Thomas' need for proof?

___

___

___

___

The key to extinguishing our enemy's flaming arrows is to know the truth of God's Word. We can also point to times in our past when God has met our needs and know that He will meet us again! More on that tomorrow!

5. What is your need today? Are Satan's arrows lies, or do you need to "only believe"? Journal what's on your heart.

___

___

___

___

___

___

___

___

day 4

standing firm in our God's faithfulness

Whatever happens, conduct yourselves in a manner worthy of the gospel of Christ. Then, whether I come and see you or only hear about you in my absence, I will know that you stand firm in the one Spirit, striving together as one for the faith of the gospel.

(PHILIPPIANS 1:27)

Standing firm in our faith is as much about believing what God *will* do as it is about remembering what He has *already* done. God is faithful. He doesn't change. What He promises to do, He will do. When we recall what He has done for us in the past (or what He did for people in the Bible), we have assurance that He will continue to care for us in our present and our future.

REMEMBERING WHAT GOD HAS ALREADY DONE

Recall the Israelites before they entered the Promised Land. The Jordan River, which was at flood stage, lay before them. God wanted the priests to take the Ark of the Covenant ahead of the people. The moment the priests who carried the ark touched the edge of the water, the Jordan stopped flowing from upstream. They carried the ark to the center of the Jordan, and all of Israel crossed over on dry land.

week 7 | standing firm in Christ

1. **Read Joshua 4:1-9, and explain what Joshua told the elders of Israel to do.**

   _____
   _____
   _____
   _____

   > *In the future, when your children ask you, "What do these stones mean?" tell them that the flow of the Jordan was cut off before the ark of the covenant of the Lord. When it crossed the Jordan, the waters of the Jordan were cut off. These stones are to be a memorial to the people of Israel forever.* (Joshua 4:6-7)

   Our children observe how we handle difficulty. Remembering God's faithfulness during our past troubles will strengthen our faith as we face current (and future) challenges. We strengthen future generations as we teach our children to do the same.

2. **What are some ways we can set up "stones of remembrance" to remind us of God's faithfulness?**

   _____
   _____
   _____
   _____
   _____
   _____

3. **Describe a situation when your faith was tested, and, later, you drew on what you learned in a subsequent trial.**

   _____
   _____
   _____
   _____
   _____

standing firm in our God's faithfulness | day 4

WHAT WE KNOW TO BE TRUE

Recalling how God helped us in the past is encouraging, for sure. But sometimes it's still hard to know how to handle what is right in front of us.

4. Write out Hebrews 11:1, and emphasize what you learn about faith.

_____
_____
_____

5. The rest of Hebrews 11 lists many people who exercised faith in the face of opposition. Who stands out to you? Why? Whom can you add to this list?

_____
_____
_____
_____
_____

6. According to Hebrews 12:1-2, how do we grow in our faith?

_____
_____
_____

God is pleased when we move forward in faith, which may be as simple as doing the next thing required in our lives. Even when we don't know how things will turn out, we trust God with the results. When our faith is weak, His faithfulness is our shield. Walking through suffering or other difficulties tests our faith. As our faith is strengthened, we are better able to face future onslaughts of enemy attack.

> *For everyone born of God is victorious and overcomes the world; and this is the victory that has conquered and overcome the world–our [continuing, persistent] faith [in Jesus the Son of God]. Who is the one who is victorious and overcomes the world? It is the one who believes and recognizes the fact that Jesus is the Son of God.* (1 John 5:4-5, AMP)

#standingfirmbiblestudy

7. Where are you struggling in your faith right now? Tell the Lord all about it.

day 5

God is completely faithful and never leaves us alone and unprotected in our spiritual battles. He strengthens us through His Word, so we can face the onslaught of enemy attack, protected by the Shield of Faith.

personal action plan

Jesus Christ is faithful and true. He encourages our mustard-seed faith and is gentle with us when we doubt. Where in your life do you struggle with faith?

_____
_____
_____
_____
_____
_____
_____

Write out Scriptures that build your faith and help you trust God.

_____
_____
_____
_____
_____

#standingfirmbiblestudy

week 7 | standing firm in Christ

Using these Scriptures, write a battlefield prayer of commitment.

Find three songs that build your faith and help you know God protects you.

week eight – the helmet of salvation

day 1 – our victorious God

day 2 – the helmet of salvation

day 3 – the enemy wants to control our minds

day 4 – standing firm with the mind of Christ

day 5 – personal action plan

week 8 | standing firm in Christ

weekly prep

This week is critical in our study. We will learn how our minds influence our actions. How we think makes a difference. Today's question is this: What do you *think* (or know) about your spiritual battle? It's not quite the same as how you *feel* about it. What phrases run through your mind?

_____
_____
_____
_____
_____
_____
_____
_____
_____
_____
_____
_____
_____
_____

day 1

our victorious, saving God

Praise be to the Lord, to God our Savior, who daily bears our burdens. (PSALM 68:19)

Victory implies a battle or a contest. In Texas high schools, victory is winning the football game under Friday night lights. For my kids, it was also winning the game against our cross-town rival. For my girls, victory meant going to winter guard state championships. Carry it forward, and it's winning the Super Bowl, the World Series, or a gold medal at the Olympics.

Our culture is fixated on winning. A quick internet search yields lists of "winning quotes."

- Paul "Bear" Bryant: "Winning isn't everything, but it beats anything that comes in second."

- Kobe Bryant: "Winning takes precedence over all. There's no gray area. No almosts."

- Tiger Woods: "Winning solves everything."

- Vince Lombardi: "Winning isn't everything; it's the only thing!"

- Unknown: "It doesn't matter if you win or lose; it's how you play the game."

But we can't win at everything. If we're gifted in athletics, with effort we may win most of the time. But life is filled with other arenas–home life, school, work, and relationships. We can win (or lose) there, as well. Our battlefields vary. Some are football fields, some are gymnasiums, and some are literal killing fields where blood is spilled to purchase freedom.

#standingfirmbiblestudy

Real victory is FREEDOM! *Ultimate* victory is freedom from the dark forces of evil in the spiritual realm. These opponents are just as real as the lineman who wears a helmet, shoulder pads and kneepads and is ready to take you down.

Our enemy is skilled at exploiting our weaknesses. His one and only goal is to leave us defeated–physically, mentally, emotionally, financially, relationally, and spiritually. He will use anything he can find to knock us off our game.

Battles can be long and arduous. Battles can be brief. Our spiritual battles may be as "simple" as maintaining a consistent quiet time or as challenging as overcoming addiction. All of them bleed into the spiritual realm. The fight for our children's souls is evident in our relationships with them. Sometimes we pray over every little thing but continually see a powerful spirit of rebellion in them.

We may feel helpless, weak, and unable to stand, but we are not destined to live in defeat. When we have done everything we know to stand firm (Ephesians 6:13), we keep standing. Then God shows up, exercising His power on our behalf. This is how we fight our spiritual battles. God wins every time. When He wins, we win!

THE GOD OF OUR SALVATION

David wrote Psalm 68. Its exact occasion is unknown, but this psalm celebrates victory. It opens with praise to God and then recounts some of Israel's historic victories. It ends with the anticipation of future victory and all the kingdoms of the earth worshiping God. Tucked in there is this gem:

Praise be to the Lord, to God our Savior, who daily bears our burdens. (Psalm 68:19)

Isaiah says:

Surely God is my salvation; I will trust and not be afraid. (Isaiah 12:2)

In these verses, *el* is paired with *yeshua (*which means "salvation, deliverance, help, victory, prosperity,")[20] giving us this Name of God:

el yeshua: GOD OF SALVATION

In Psalms it is GOD OF OUR SALVATION. In Isaiah it is the personal GOD OF MY SALVATION.

When we look at our world today, it's easy to think God is not watching. That He doesn't care. That He's not really in control. Nothing could be further from the truth. God *is* watching. And when it's time to fight, He wins! He fought for Israel, He fights for us, and He equips us to fight. Remember what we learned on our very first day?

When Pharaoh finally released the Israelites, they packed up all their belongings and began the trek to Canaan. After they left, Pharaoh realized he had just lost all his slave labor. So, he pursued them to bring them back to Egypt.

Meanwhile, the Israelites came upon the Red Sea. When they realized that Pharaoh's army had followed them, they panicked! Would they be captured and enslaved again by their Egyptian taskmasters? Would they die in the desert? God's plan for them was victory! Moses told the people:

> *Do not be afraid. Stand firm and you will see the deliverance the LORD will bring you today. The Egyptians you see today you will never see again. The LORD will fight for you; you need only to be still.* (Exodus 14:13-14)

Did you catch that? The Israelites were to stand firm and watch God fight for them! God opened the Red Sea, and the Israelites crossed over on dry land. When Pharaoh's army followed them through, the waters crashed over them, drowning every single soldier (Exodus 14).

When the Israelites finally entered the Promised Land, they were ready to capture the city of Jericho. God's plan there was victory as well. But the execution was a little different. Instead of having them march through the city gates with drawn swords, God told them to march around the city one time each day for six days, with each priest carrying a ram's horn. On the seventh day, the priests gave a long, loud blast on their horns, and then all the Israelites shouted. Immediately following that, the walls collapsed, and the Israelites marched in and took the town (Joshua 6).

> We may feel helpless, weak, and unable to stand, but we are not destined for defeat When we have done everything we know to stand firm (Ephesians 6:13), God shows up, exercising His strength on our behalf. This is how we fight our spiritual battles. God wins every time. When He wins, we win!

This is our victorious God! God's plan is for each of us to experience salvation, as well. He doesn't want us trapped and held captive by anything or anyone.

JESUS IS THE VICTOR

Jesus, although He was fully God, was also fully human (Colossians 1:19). He experienced the gamut of pain and suffering and was tempted in all the ways that we are (Hebrews 4:15). He knows what it's like to face subtle temptation, and He knows what it's like to face it head-on. With only a word, Jesus cast out demons everywhere He went. He had authority over them and they knew it. When He told them to leave, they obeyed.

Jesus told his disciples they would experience trials and sorrows, but they didn't need to worry, because He had overcome the world! (John 16:33)

He was betrayed and handed over to Roman soldiers, who beat, tortured, and eventually crucified Him. Those watching thought that was the end. The One who healed the sick, made the lame walk, caused the blind to see, cast out demons, and even raised the dead back to life, hung lifeless on the cross. Friends buried Him in a tomb. Oh, the grief. It was beyond their ability to understand. But three days later, He rose from that tomb–conquering death! Jesus claimed victory over the grave! Because of His victory, we have eternal life! (1 Corinthians 15:57)

THE HOLY SPIRIT IS THE KEY TO VICTORIOUS LIVING

Late one night, a Pharisee named Nicodemus visited Jesus. He had some burning questions he needed answers for. But because he was part of Israel's religious leadership, it would look questionable if he approached Jesus during the day. When Nicodemus founds Jesus, he said to him, "We know you are a teacher who has come from God" (John 3:2).

I love that Nicodemus says *we know*. This tells me he and his other Pharisee friends were talking about Jesus and concluded that Jesus was sent from God. But rather than follow this topic, Jesus got straight to the point (as He always does). He told Nicodemus that no one could see the Kingdom of God unless they were born again. This puzzled Nicodemus, so Jesus explained.

> *Jesus answered, "Very truly I tell you, no one can enter the kingdom of God unless they are born of water and the Spirit. Flesh gives birth to flesh, but the Spirit gives birth to spirit."* (John 3:5-6)

To be saved (or born again) requires a spiritual birth, which is brought about by the Holy Spirit, who generates spiritual life and takes up residence in our very souls (2 Corinthians 1:22). The Holy Spirit is the key to living a victorious Christian life.

In the Old Testament, Israel did not keep God's law. Once the Israelites possessed the Promised Land, they cycled through sin and deliverance for many hundreds of years. The Book of Judges chronicles their history before they had kings. The Books of 1 and 2 Kings and 1 and 2 Chronicles record their history of good kings and bad kings. When a good king rose to power, they worshiped God for a short time. When bad kings reigned, they worshiped the gods of neighboring nations and followed their unholy religious customs. All this revealed Israel's need for a Savior and a way to help them obey God.

The Holy Spirit is God's answer to Israel's need for help in obeying Him. He told the prophet Ezekiel:

> *I will give you a new heart and put a new spirit in you; I will remove from you your heart of stone and give you a heart of flesh. And I will put my Spirit in you and move you to follow my decrees and be careful to keep my laws.* (Ezekiel 36:26-27)

Because of the Holy Spirit's presence in our lives and our submission to Him, we are *moved* to walk in obedience to God's Word. The words *be careful to keep* mean "to guard, to be careful ... to watch carefully over, to be on one's guard."[21] We are to be like a soldier standing guard at night, watching for anyone or anything that might intrude upon his camp.

The Holy Spirit gives us the desire to be diligent over our spiritual lives. When we are aware of our weaknesses, we may choose not to take part in activities where it could be hard for us to honor our convictions. When temptation comes to attend such events, the Holy Spirit gently (or sometimes strongly!) convicts us and gives us strength to say no. We know that participating in these activities puts us in a place of vulnerability. We diligently watch over our lives.

This is on-purpose living. It's being diligent to follow what God calls us to do and be, and what He calls us *not* to do and *not* to be.

THE FINAL VICTORY

Toward the end of his life, the apostle John was exiled to the Greek island of Patmos. While John was there, God gave him a vision of end times. The Book of Revelation results from that vision. Chapters 2-3 are messages to the seven churches that represented early Christianity. Most of the letters follow the same pattern. Christ commends them for things they did well and then confronts them and calls them to repentance in areas where they became lax. He ends each message with a promise to those who are victorious. The messages given to these churches, including their rebukes, commendations, and promises, are for us too.

The believers in *Ephesus* did not tolerate false teaching. They worked hard and persevered in their faith. But they did it through the lens of legalism, not because of their deep love for Christ. For those who repented and returned to their first love, Christ would give *the right to eat from the tree of life* (Revelation 2:1-7).

Christ commended the believers in *Smyrna*. He encouraged them not to be afraid of what they would soon suffer, even persecution that led to death. To those who suffered imprisonment and persecution, Christ would give *the victor's crown*, or *the crown of life* (Revelation 2:8-11).

Pergamum was an evil city, filled with false teaching that led to sexual immorality and eating food sacrificed to idols. Some of its believers followed those teachings. To those who repented, Christ would give some of the *hidden manna,* which may refer to the manna the Israelites ate while wandering in the wilderness. It may also refer to Christ as the Bread of Life. They would also receive a *white stone with a new name written on it, known only to the one who receives it* (Revelation 2:12-17).

Many of the believers in *Thyatira* also tolerated false teaching and Satanic influence that led to sexual immorality. Their teachings were disguised as "Satan's so-called deep secrets" (Revelation 2:24). Christ encouraged the faithful to hold on to the truth. Those who were faithful would *rule with Him and receive the morning star* (Revelation 2:26-28). The morning star is another name for Christ (Revelation 22:16).

The church in *Sardis* had believers with weak faith. Christ challenged the believers to wake up and strengthen their faith. The victorious would be *dressed in white and their names would never be removed from the book of life* (Revelation 3:1-6).

The believers in *Philadelphia* were discerning. They knew the difference between true and false teachers and did not deny Christ's Name. Those who held on to the truth would be *pillars in God's temple and would have Christ's new name written on them* (Revelation 3:7-13).

The Christians in *Laodicea* were lukewarm, but they didn't know it. They became immersed in the culture of their day. To those who would repent and overcome, Christ would give *the right to sit with Him on His throne* (Revelation 3:14-22).

It's easy to look at the problem areas with these churches and think, *Wow, they had major problems!* In reality, all of us struggle with these issues. At one time or another, we have lost our "first love" toward God. We may not be involved in sexual immorality or eat food sacrificed to idols, but when have we ignored the Holy Spirit's prompting in our lives to set aside an unwholesome habit? When have we chosen not to strengthen our faith? The messages to the churches are messages to each of us individually, along with the call to repent and follow Christ wholeheartedly.

These rebukes are not a threat for the loss of salvation. Our eternity with Christ is secure. These promises are encouragement to **stand firm** in the truth that we know, with our eyes fixed on Christ as our future reward. Look at all these promises!

1. *The right to eat from the tree of life* (Revelation 2:1-7).
2. *The victor's crown, or the crown of life* (Revelation 2:8-11).
3. *Hidden manna and a new name* (Revelation 2:12-17).
4. *To rule with Christ and receive the morning star* (Revelation 2:26-28).
5. *To be dressed in white; their names will never be removed from the Book of Life* (Revelation 3:1-6).
6. *To be pillars in God's temple and have Christ's new name written on them* (Revelation 3:7-13).
7. *To sit with Christ on His throne* (Revelation 3:14-22).

Finally, we get to the end of the Book. Satan is bound for a thousand years while Christ reigns on earth. The devil is released for a brief time for one final battle. Nations march against Jerusalem, ready to consume it. But God sends fire from heaven to devour them. And then our enemy is cast into the "lake of burning sulfur" to be tormented day and night, forever (Revelation 20).

God makes all things new, and we spend eternity with Him. No more sin. No more sorrow. No more tears. While we actively wait for this ultimate victory, let's join the Apostle Paul, who said:

> *I press on toward the goal to win the prize for which God has called me heavenward in Christ Jesus.* (Philippians 3:14)

> ***Going Deeper:*** *In BibleGateway search for* God salvation *(without quotes) and see the many verses that proclaim this name of our victorious God!*

day 2

the helmet of salvation

Take the helmet of salvation and the sword of the Spirit, which is the word of God.
(EPHESIANS 6:17)

When our children were small, my husband and I did our best to form their thoughts about food. To get them to try something different, we didn't always tell them what we had prepared. For a while we got away with it. Once they were older, however, it became more difficult. They had preconceived ideas about how certain foods would taste and whether they would like them. We could not change their minds, no matter how creative we were. Not until *they* changed their minds was there any hope they would try something different.

Shepherd's pie is a favorite comfort food for our family. In case you're not familiar with it: It's a casserole, of sorts, a combination of ground beef and veggies topped with mashed potatoes, all baked until bubbly. In recent years, my husband and I have chosen not to eat potatoes. One winter evening I made this meal, but instead of mashed potatoes topping the pie, I used seasoned mashed cauliflower. After a grueling winter guard rehearsal, Abigail came home famished! She sat down with her dinner, expecting to enjoy her favorite veggie. What she got was something different. And the reaction is something we'll never forget. Drama and gagging! She had decided that cauliflower would never replace potatoes. And she saw through my disguise.

Occasionally, however, our kids would spend the night at a friend's house and come home raving about something new they had eaten. What changed? Their thoughts about a new food.

#standingfirmbiblestudy

week 8 | standing firm in Christ

OUR THOUGHT LIFE DETERMINES HOW WE FIGHT

How we think about things makes a difference. Thinking deeply is good. Thinking a long time about something can also be good. But our thinking becomes unhealthy when we begin to obsess or when we allow our thoughts to dwell on something that is sinful. The more we think about it, the more it becomes part of us, or enters our hearts. Paul knew this, so he encouraged the Ephesians to protect their minds with the Helmet of Salvation.

Since wounds to the head can be fatal, it is vital that we protect them! Our thought life impacts the way we live and how we handle our spiritual battles. Let's learn at how we can sharpen our minds, and thus "protect our heads."

1. **Read the passage below. Using different colors, underline what we are to do, put a box around what God does, and draw a circle around the benefits of obedience.**

   My son, if you accept my words and store up my commands within you, turning your ear to wisdom and applying your heart to understanding–indeed, if you call out for insight and cry aloud for understanding, and if you look for it as for silver and search for it as for hidden treasure, then you will understand the fear of the LORD and find the knowledge of God. For the LORD gives wisdom; from his mouth come knowledge and understanding. He holds success in store for the upright, he is a shield to those whose walk is blameless, for he guards the course of the just and protects the way of his faithful ones. Then you will understand what is right and just and fair–every good path. For wisdom will enter your heart, and knowledge will be pleasant to your soul. (Proverbs 2:1-10)

2. **Summarize what you discovered.**

   _____
   _____
   _____
   _____
   _____

3. According to Proverbs 3:5-6 and Isaiah 55:8-9, in our thinking, what should we always be aware of?

___

SALVATION MEANS VICTORY!

The word *helmet* is used only twice in the New Testament–in Ephesians 6:17 and in 1 Thessalonians 5:8.

> *But since we belong to the day, let us be sober, putting on faith and love as a breastplate, and the hope of salvation as a helmet.* (1 Thessalonians 5:8)

4. Read 1 Thessalonians 5:6-11. What is the context for our "hope of salvation"?

___

Verse 9 tells us that God did not appoint us to suffer His wrath. In the heat of battle, we are not destined for defeat. We may pray that God delivers us *from* the battle. More importantly is the promise that God will deliver (or save) us *through* our spiritual battles. Paul knew that how we think about our battles impacts our hope and how we experience victory. For both the Breastplate of Righteousness and the Helmet of Salvation, he refers to an Old Testament Scripture from Isaiah that describes God as a warrior fighting for His people.

> *He put on righteousness as his breastplate, and the helmet of salvation on his head; he put on the garments of vengeance and wrapped himself in zeal as in a cloak.* (Isaiah 59:17)

Isaiah 59 describes Israel's deep fall into sin. He identifies with his people as he describes their depravity, which was so great they could not rescue themselves. Their sin was like darkness in

#standingfirmbiblestudy

the middle of the day. God alone was strong enough to save them. He goes to war for them, bringing redemption and salvation to the nation.

We, too, have God's righteousness as our body armor and His salvation as our head protection. He is our hope of salvation as we engage in spiritual battle! Ultimately, our "hope of salvation" is eternity with God, not eternal separation from Him.

day 3

the enemy wants to control our minds

In his pride the wicked man does not seek him; in all his thoughts there is no room for God.
(PSALM 10:4)

The brain has many functions. Everything we do (physically, emotionally, and mentally) stems from somewhere in the brain–the "control center" of our lives. The five senses and their responses are rooted deep within the brain. It controls our physical movements, heart rate, and breathing. Our thoughts, emotions, and memories are hidden inside our brains. Certain parts of the brain secrete hormones that affect mood, metabolism, and other physiological responses. Our brains are beautifully complex. But our brains are not the same as our minds.

What do our minds do? The basic function of the mind is to *think*! Most of how our brain controls our bodies is automatic. We don't "think" in order to breathe. Although, when anxiety hits, we may *think our way through* deep breathing exercises. We don't tell our hearts to beat or our blood to flow.

Many of our thoughts, however, do trigger some brain functions, especially those related to memory and mood. The process of thinking affects much of our lives. If the enemy of our souls can control our thinking process, then he can control our physical lives and our effectiveness for the Lord, causing us to become frustrated and spin around in defeat. That's why it's essential to recognize when Satan is at work so we can battle and regain control of our thought life.

week 8 | standing firm in Christ

1. **Read Philippians 4:1-3. Now, in Philippians 2:1-5 below, underline any word that relates to unity.**

   Therefore if you have any encouragement from being united with Christ, if any comfort from his love, if any common sharing in the Spirit, if any tenderness and compassion, then make my joy complete by being like-minded, having the same love, being one in spirit and of one mind. Do nothing out of selfish ambition or vain conceit. Rather, in humility value others above yourselves, not looking to your own interests but each of you to the interests of the others. In your relationships with one another, have the same mindset as Christ Jesus. (Philippians 2:1-5)

   How many did you find? If you look in your Bible, you'll see that Paul tells the Philippians to live in unity *five times in only two verses*. Then in verse five, he explains that this unity is to look like Jesus Christ.

2. **Using what you just read, along with Philippians 4:2 as a cross-reference, describe the tool Satan used in the church at Philippi and Paul's instructions for overcoming the damage.**

   _____
   _____
   _____
   _____

   Sometimes good things become the enemy of the best things, even thoughts about good things. But if God has called you to do something, yet you are reluctant to follow through, maybe Satan is distracting you with other good things. He does not want you to be effective for God! He may settle for "a little effectiveness over here" at the expense of "huge impact over there."

3. **What does the above paragraph speak to your heart? How might you have experienced "a little effectiveness" at the expense of "huge impact"?**

   _____
   _____
   _____

the enemy wants to control our minds | day 3

Satan uses various ways to make us ineffective for the Lord. The following "tools" are specific to how he gets into our heads to keep us from the life and love of God. Consider the following "tools" Satan uses to control our minds.

Worry & Anxiety	Proverbs 12:25; Matthew 6:25-34
Depression	1 Kings 19:1-4; Jeremiah 20:14, 18
Doubt	James 1:6; Judges 6:12, 14-17, 36-40
Anger & Bitterness	Psalm 37:8; Ecclesiastes 7:9; 1 Peter 3:9
Jealousy & Envy	Proverbs 14:30; Psalm 37:1-3
Busyness	Psalm 39:6; Psalms 127:2
Pride	Proverbs 21:4; Psalm 10:4

4. **Has Satan used any of these "tools" to control your mind? Does he use one more effectively than others? Journal about it.**

_____
_____
_____
_____
_____

Have you ever examined the ground of an unplowed field? It's hard and dry. If it is to be used for growing vegetation, it must be broken up and turned over. The moisture from below needs to be brought to the surface. Weeds need to be pulled. Sometimes nutrients and more moisture need to be added. The heart and attitude of a proud person is much like a dry, unplowed field. Proud people often don't listen to others. Their minds are made up.

Haughty eyes and a proud heart–the unplowed field of the wicked–produce sin.
(Proverbs 21:4)

Wicked people are not the only ones who can have a heart like an unplowed field. Christians can, too. We get to choose. Will we allow the Holy Spirit to dig it up so He can use our lives for His glory?

#standingfirmbiblestudy

5. **Are there any unplowed areas in your life that the Holy Spirit wants to "turn over" and prepare for work He wants you to do? Are any areas "off limits" to the Holy Spirit? Remember, He wants you to produce a crop well over what He sows!**

_____
_____
_____
_____
_____

day 4

standing firm in victory with the mind of Christ

We demolish arguments and every pretension that sets itself up against the knowledge of God, and we take captive every thought to make it obedient to Christ. (2 Corinthians 10:5)

When we teach our young teenagers how to drive, we instruct them to focus straight ahead. Yes, they glance from side to side and in the rearview mirror, but their focus should be directly in front of them. If they shift their focus to a group of deer grazing by the side of the road, their minds tell them to turn the steering wheel in that direction.

Similarly, once Eve thought about the forbidden fruit, she stopped thinking about the good things God provided for her enjoyment. *Eve shifted her focus*. Her extended conversation with the serpent increased her appetite for what she couldn't have. Eventually, Eve fulfilled her fleshly desires.

God designed our minds to work in this manner. Our lives follow the paths that our thoughts take. We must submit control of our minds to the Holy Spirit and not let our thoughts wander aimlessly. The more we do so, the less likely we are to fall into sin.

THE BATTLE FOR THE MIND

Whenever we encounter something that disagrees with Scripture (our thoughts or someone else's), our job is to pause, identify the truth, and stand firmly in it. People may challenge us with direct opposition. Other times, opposition may be more subtle. In addition, we should be aware when our emotions lie to us. Fear, anxiety, disillusionment, and frustration can wreak havoc on our thought lives. Our responsibility is to "take captive" all these thoughts and bring them into submission to Christ.

Let's examine 2 Corinthians 10:5 in detail.

> *We demolish arguments and every pretension that sets itself up against the knowledge of God, and we take captive every thought to make it obedient to Christ.* (2 Corinthians 10:5)

1. **Paul instructs us what to do with anything that sets itself up against the knowledge of God. What are some examples of arguments and pretension that we are to oppose?**

   _____
   _____
   _____
   _____

Arguments are rarely productive. Pretense is anything made up. It can be a false teaching, but it can also be a convincing lie. As believers, we must discern the difference between truth and lies.

2. **When have you had to take your thoughts captive?**

   _____
   _____
   _____
   _____

3. **How do you make your thoughts obedient to Christ?**

   _____
   _____
   _____

This is what "taking thoughts captive" looks like for me.

Sometimes I wonder what it would be like if I were a better-known writer. This thought results from pride. Scripture is clear that God opposes the proud but gives grace to the humble (James 4:6). The only name worth elevating is the Name of Jesus (Philippians 2:9-11). My job is to share whatever message God gives me. It's His job to see to it that the right people hear that message at the right time. The goal is to share the gospel of peace so many are freed and reconciled to God. I am simply an instrument.

If I'm angry with someone, it's easy for me to have (not-so-nice) conversations with my steering wheel. When I recognize this, I remember that God forgave me for all *my* sins (1 John 1:9), and He wants me to forgive *anyone* with whom I have a grievance (Matthew 18:21-22).

Even though the Bible leaves no room for disagreement, many of the youth in our culture, including Christians, have an inaccurate understanding of what is acceptable behavior. I have friends of different religions and friends who don't believe one word of the Bible. These thoughts and belief systems run contrary to Scripture. When given the opportunity, we speak the truth–in love.

I don't always agree with everything I hear in conversations. I am not a quick thinker, so I'm not always ready to make a defense. Usually, I choose to be quiet, go home, and do some research. I learn the truth to ensure that I am thinking properly about what I heard. Then I'm ready to speak the truth if I have an opportunity to do so later.

Renewing Our Minds

Before we know Christ, we live and think in a certain way. Paul calls this our "old nature." We might live a moral life, but it's not motivated by a desire to please God. When we come to Christ, however, we receive a "new nature," which is created to be like God (Ephesians 4:24). This "becoming" does not happen overnight. It's a process that takes time. In fact, it isn't completed until we meet the Lord face to face (Philippians 1:6).

1. **According to Romans 12:1-2 and Ephesians 4:23, what are Christians to do with their minds?**

_____

_____

_____

week 8 | standing firm in Christ

2. Read the verses below. Underline how we renew, or cleanse, our minds.

Husbands, love your wives, just as Christ loved the church and gave himself up for her to make her holy, cleansing her by the washing with water through the word. (Ephesians 5:25-26)

But when the kindness and love of God our Savior appeared, he saved us, not because of righteous things we had done, but because of his mercy. He saved us through the washing of rebirth and renewal by the Holy Spirit. (Titus 3:4-5)

Yesterday we looked at some ways Satan tries to muddle our minds. Below is an updated version of the chart and corresponding Scriptures with ways we can renew our minds.

Worry & Anxiety	Peace	Psalm 55:22; Isaiah 26:3-4
Depression	Hope	Deuteronomy 31:8; Romans 15:13; Psalm 33:18
Doubt	Faith	Matthew 17:20; Hebrews 12:2
Anger & Bitterness	Forgiveness	Ephesians 4:31-32; Colossians 3:12-13
Jealousy & Envy	Contentment	2 Corinthians 12:9-10; Psalms 34:10b
Busyness	Stillness/Trust	Exodus 14:14; Psalm 46:10; Isaiah 32:17
Pride	Humility	Psalm 25:9; 149:4; James 4:6

3. Consider your spiritual battles. Are you susceptible to any of the attitudes above? If so, look up the Scriptures to renew your mind. Include additional Scriptures if you have them. Then journal your thoughts below.

_____
_____
_____
_____
_____
_____
_____

THE MIND / HEART CONNECTION

Our minds and our hearts work together. The more we think about something, the more we believe it. Our actions indicate what we truly believe. Good or bad, the shift from mind to heart is where life change occurs. Any time we interact with Scripture, we use our minds. Whether we listen to a podcast, read our Bibles or a devotional, meditate or memorize Scripture, participate in a Bible study, talk about it, or pray with a friend, we use our minds. How we approach these activities indicates our hearts toward God.

4. **Write out Matthew 22:37. Evaluate your time in God's presence. Do you need to make any adjustments?**

_____
_____
_____
_____
_____
_____
_____
_____
_____

Our minds are powerful, and it takes more than a little oomph to change them, especially when a belief or thought pattern has taken root. When a negative thought pattern gets started, we need to recognize it as soon as possible. The longer we dwell on something, the more ingrained it becomes in our lives. When we have a deeply rooted thought pattern, it may take a while for our minds to shift. We must continually replace our negative thoughts with positive thoughts. Sound familiar? Like speaking truth over lies, we read Scripture that speaks to our situation, repeatedly (and aloud!) if necessary, until the truth takes root and the lies are removed.

We can change our hearts by changing our minds.

The battle for the mind is purposed, not passive. If we want to experience life change, we must actively guard and renew our minds with God's Word. When we do so, God's Word will take root in our hearts and we will be able to stand firm in the victory that is ours in Christ Jesus.

day 5

Satan wants power over us by controlling our minds, but God has victory in store for us! With the Helmet of Salvation, we take every thought captive and make it obedient to Christ, renewing our minds through consistent time in the Word of God.

personal action plan

Jesus Christ is the Victor, and He wants us to live victorious lives. We want to think like Jesus. How does He want you to think about your spiritual battle?

_____
_____
_____
_____
_____

Consider the heart/mind connection. How does your thought life influence how you feel about your spiritual battle?

_____
_____
_____
_____
_____
_____
_____
_____

#standingfirmbiblestudy

week 8 | standing firm in Christ

Write out Scriptures that renew your mind so you can have thoughts that reflect the mind of Christ.

_____
_____
_____
_____
_____
_____
_____
_____

Using these Scriptures, write a battlefield prayer of commitment.

_____
_____
_____
_____
_____
_____
_____
_____
_____
_____
_____
_____

Find three songs that renew your mind.

_____
_____
_____

in conclusion

Remember, we won't always stand; but the One who enables us to stand also lifts us up and sets us on a rock where we can stand firm once again (Psalm 40:2). As you may have discovered, all the pieces of armor are connected. Each one supports the others. Truth keeps us from getting tangled up in a life of lies. But truth also protects our minds and our hearts. When the enemy attacks our minds, the truth sends him running away. The cure for doubt is faith. When our minds are fraught with worry, the Prince of Peace helps us focus on truth. We have righteousness not by anything we do, but through faith. Through the power of the Holy Spirit, we can walk in obedience to all God calls us to. When we meditate on Scripture, truth moves from our minds to our hearts and we experience life change. This, my friend, is a life of victory. Below is a summary of some questions we can ask as we face and evaluate our spiritual battles.

Belt of Truth	What lies does the enemy want me to believe about my battle? What is the *truth* from God's Word about my battle?
Breastplate of Righteousness	What do my thoughts, words, and actions *reveal about my heart*? Where do I *need to yield* to the Holy Spirit's leadership in my battle?
Firm Foundation of the Gospel of Peace	Is there someone in my battle with whom I need to *reconcile*? How does Satan *disrupt my peace* in my battle?
Shield of Faith	How am I *tempted to doubt* God's plan in my battle? How has God met my needs in the past? Do I trust Him to meet me now?
Helmet of Salvation	How do my *thoughts* affect my spiritual battle? Which thoughts need to come under the authority of Jesus Christ?

We want to grow habits that help us face our spiritual battles strategically. God gives us the power to stand firm in who Christ is, and who we are in Him. As we wear ALL of God's armor (Ephesians 6:11 and 13), which is wrapped up in Christ's character, we have everything we need to stand firm against our enemy and experience victory!

#standingfirmbiblestudy

week 8 | standing firm in Christ

stand firm declarations

CHRIST is our truth.
Jesus answered, "I am the way and the truth and the life. No one comes to the Father except through me." (John 14:6)

CHRIST is our righteousness.
And be found in him, not having a righteousness of my own that comes from the law, but that which is through faith in Christ–the righteousness that comes from God on the basis of faith. (Philippians 3:9)

CHRIST is our peace.
Peace I leave with you; my peace I give you. I do not give to you as the world gives. Do not let your hearts be troubled and do not be afraid. (John 14:27)

CHRIST is our victory and salvation.
But thanks be to God! He gives us the victory through our Lord Jesus Christ. (1 Corinthians 15:57)

CHRIST took our place and suffered the death we should have suffered. He is our shield.
The LORD is my strength and my shield; my heart trusts in him, and he helps me. My heart leaps for joy, and with my song I praise him. (Psalm 28:7)

CHRIST is our sword.
In the beginning was the Word, and the Word was with God, and the Word was God. (John 1:1)

For the word of God is alive and active. Sharper than any double-edged sword, it penetrates even to dividing soul and spirit, joints and marrow; it judges the thoughts and attitudes of the heart. (Hebrews 4:12)

Holy Father,

How I thank you for providing everything we need to stand firm against our enemy. May we walk in integrity and always speak truthfully. Help us not to believe the lies of the enemy. Instead, remind us of the truth from Your Word so we can discern truth from error. Fill us with the Holy Spirit. We submit our desires to Your desires. Enable us to follow You in obedience from a heart of love. May we be peacemakers, not those who stir up strife. May we always be ready to share the gospel as You provide opportunities. You are our Shield. You protect us in our trials. We know You are greater than anything that comes against us. Grow our faith as we learn to trust You. May we abide in You and Your Word. As we stand firm in who You are, may we stand firm against our enemy. You are everything we need to experience victory.

In Jesus's Name, Amen.

appendix

how to use biblegateway

how to study one verse

meet Jesus!

about the author

endnotes

how to use biblegateway

There are many wonderful websites that can enrich your study of God's Word. I use BibleGateway quite often. This "mini manual" will show you how I use some of its basic functions. It's written for desktop or laptop computers, not cell phones or the app.

BibleGateway is found at this web address: https://biblegateway.com

VERSE OR PASSAGE LOOK-UP

The most basic function in BibleGateway is to look up a verse or passage of Scripture. At the top of the home page, simply enter the Bible verse or passage you want to read, select your desired translation, and click the magnifying glass or hit enter.

Once the verse or passage is displayed, you have some additional options. I will highlight three.

- The **parallel translation** icon looks like two pieces of paper next to each other. Selecting this allows you to display up to five translations side-by-side.

- The **gear icon** lets you choose what you want displayed with the text: footnotes, cross-references, verse numbers, headings, and red letter. I find the cross-references particularly useful. I don't always have them highlighted, however. Sometimes I want to copy and paste just the verses. When cross-references are selected, they are displayed as superscripts within the biblical text. Clicking on one brings up a small window with all related verses. You can scroll through them or navigate directly to the verses by clicking the reference.

- The **read-aloud** icon looks like a speaker or a megaphone.

Compare One Verse in Multiple Translations

One of my favorite ways to use BibleGateway is to compare translations for a single verse. Type in the reference for one verse only at the top of the home page and click the magnifying glass or hit enter. Below the biblical text and any footnotes for your verse you will see something like this:

<u>John 15:1 in all English translations</u>

Clicking this brings up a new screen with your verse in over 50 translations. You can quickly see the different ways your verse is translated, giving you additional insight into your selected verse.

Concordance Look-up

On the home page, type in a word or phrase of interest; for example, the word *anxiety*. BibleGateway will display every verse where the word *anxiety* is used in your selected translation.

You can also search for a phrase by placing it in quotation marks. If you search for the phrase "stand firm," BibleGateway will display all verses with this exact phrase.

You can also search for multiple words within a verse. If you search for stand firm (without quotations), BibleGateway will include all verses that have both words in the verse, including variations of the word *stand*: *stands* and *standing*.

Both are helpful. You might want to search for verses that have the words *stand* and *fall* in the same verse. BibleGateway will do this for you.

In a column to the right of your search results, BibleGateway filters your results by Old and New Testament and by book of the Bible.

Topical Study

The best way I've found for studying topics on BibleGateway is to start with one verse or passage you know covers your topic.

Philippians 4:6-7 is the first passage that comes to mind when I think about the topic of worry or anxiety. After you type the passage reference in the search bar and click on the magnifying glass or hit enter, the passage is displayed. Above and to the right of the passage display window are three options. Click on STUDY. BibleGateway displays a column of resources for additional study. Resources marked with "Plus" are included in BibleGateway's paid subscription.

Scroll to the bottom and you'll see the *Dictionary of Bible Themes*. This is one of my favorite resources. Clicking it brings up over 30 categories related to Philippians 4:6-7, including topics such as renewal, refuge, stress, suffering, comfort, depression, and many others. Clicking one of these brings up all the Scripture references tied to it. You can navigate to each verse by clicking its reference.

BibleGateway offers many other study resources. These are the ones I use the most and think you will find the most helpful.

BibleGateway is used with permission.

how to study one verse

Do your best to present yourself to God as one approved, a worker who does not need to be ashamed and who correctly handles the word of truth. (2 TIMOTHY 2:15)

Think of someone you know really well. How did that relationship grow? Is there someone you would like to get to know better? What do you do to make that happen? The answer to both is the same. When you want to get to know someone better, you spend them with him or her. When you are together, you ask questions. You explore each other's interests. If you experience something special together, that bonds you even closer.

The same thing happens when you spend time in God's Word. Reading a verse or a passage is the "appointment." The questions you ask of the text are the conversation. The more "appointments" you have (or the more times you read through a passage), and the more questions you ask (or the more conversations you have), the better acquainted you become.

Later, when life gets sticky, the Holy Spirit will remind you of your previous conversations. Like a phone call or text at just the right time, the Scripture the Holy Spirit brings to mind will be God's words for your situation. Your relationship with Him and His Word will deepen. His Word will become even more dear–because you *know* it and it met your need at just the right time.

There are many methods for Bible study and lots of questions you can ask when reading your Bible. Two books that grounded me in Bible study are Kay Arthur's *How to Study Your Bible*[22] and Howard Hendricks' *Living by The Book*[23]. The instructions I'm giving here are found in those books. They are basic, however, and can be found in many other Bible study methods books.

You may do all of this in one sitting, and that's fine. However, if we are looking to deepen our relationship with God and His Word, specifically the verse(s) we are studying, we need to visit them often. A lengthy visit is great! But one long visit a best friend does not make. With that in mind, try to spread this out over a few days. For a passage, that's easier to do. For a verse or two, it may be challenging. But remember, we want to interact with these verses ***a lot over time***! Let's dig in!

Day One–Basics

The first step is to identify the verse or verses you want to study and answer why you chose them. We will look at 2 Timothy 3:16-17 because we are studying the power of God's Word. Plus, these two verses give us some meat to chew on regarding this topic.

1. **Write these verses in the space below.**

   _____
   _____
   _____
   _____

Next, we need to get the big picture. Studying one or two verses without looking at what's around them can get us into trouble when it comes to interpretation. We want to be sure we know what's going before those two verses. We can start with two simple questions.

2. **Who wrote it? And to whom was it written?** If you're not sure, go back to the first verses of the first chapter.

   _____
   _____
   _____

Next, look at the chapter these verses are in.

3. **What's going on?**

   _____
   _____
   _____

standing firm in Christ

Chapter 3 has two sections. The first is a warning to steer clear of "depraved people" who influence gullible people. The second section begins a "final charge" to Timothy. Paul contrasts the actions of the godly with the actions of those listed above. He then encourages Timothy to continue growing in his faith and all he learned in the Scriptures. Paul is preparing Timothy for the big take-away.

Day Two—Who and What

Let's look more carefully at the verses themselves now. Read your verses again. Do you see anyone referenced in these verses? If so, *who*?

I've found that when I ask and answer a question, especially if it seems like a rudimentary question, I like to ask a follow-up question. We see that God is mentioned in this verse. The follow-up question is:

4. What is significant about God in these verses?

_____
_____
_____
_____

He "breathed" Scripture. What in the world does that mean? Good question!

5. Are there any other "who's" in these verses?

_____
_____
_____
_____

6. **What are we talking about? In other words, what is the subject? The topic?**

___

Day Three—More Details and Why?

Read your verses again!

7. **What other details do these verses give us about our subject?**

___

8. **Use an English dictionary to define any words you're having difficulty understanding.**

___

9. **Why is this important?** Whenever you see the words "so that" or "therefore" you can almost always guarantee they answer the question *why*?

___

At this point, it's nice to look at other translations and see if you gain additional insight. BibleGateway is my favorite, but Bible Hub, Blue Letter Bible, and YouVersion are other good resources. Note any differences or added insight you find.

_____
_____
_____
_____

Day Four–Cross-References

Read your verses again!

Today we will look at cross-references. I listed the words that have a cross-reference from the NIV.

God-breathed	2 Peter 1:20-21
Teaching	Romans 4:23-24
Training in righteousness	Deuteronomy 29:29
Man of God	1 Timothy 6:11
Every good work	2 Timothy 2:21

Now that you've taken a deep look at these verses, write how these words influence the way you look at God's Word. Did you learn anything? How will you think differently?

10. Write 2 Timothy 3:16-17 in your own words.

_____
_____
_____
_____

_____

_____

_____

_____

You may feel that this was a labor-intense exercise, but I bet if I asked you to tell me what this verse says, you would come very close to having it right. Better than that, you know what this verse means. Each day you interacted with these verses, you got to know them a little better. It takes several days to memorize something, anyway.

Now it's your turn to do it on your own. If you choose a passage, it will take longer. But the more you dig into Scripture in this way, the better you will know it. And when you know it well, the Holy Spirit can bring it to the surface when you need it. You don't have to ask these questions in a particular order. But as you drill down a little at a time, you will unlock the meaning there.

meet Jesus!

The Bible tells us that God loves us and wants us to experience a full and meaningful life.

> *For God so loved the world that he gave his one and only Son.* (John 3:16)

> *I have come that they may have life, and have it to the full.* (John 10:10)

But God is perfect and holy. Sin (the wrong things we think, say, and do) separates us from God and the light and life He desires for us.

> *For all have sinned and fall short of the glory of God.* (Romans 3:23)
> *For the wages of sin is death* [eternal separation from God]. (Romans 6:23a)

> *When Jesus spoke again to the people, he said, "I am the light of the world. Whoever follows me will never walk in darkness, but will have the light of life."* (John 8:12)

Without Christ, we stumble through life as though in darkness. But we don't have to live this way. God sent His one and only Son, Jesus, into our world.

> *The Word became flesh and made his dwelling among us. We have seen his glory, the glory of the one and only Son, who came from the Father, full of grace and truth.* (John 1:14)

> *For God so loved the world that he gave his one and only Son, that whoever believes in him shall not perish but have eternal life.* (John 3:16)

Jesus lived a perfect life, and His death on the cross and subsequent resurrection from the grave satisfied our holy God's requirement for the punishment of sin. Jesus willingly gave His life for us. When we accept this as a gift from God, we begin a new relationship with Him.

> *But the gift of God is eternal life in Christ Jesus our Lord.* (Romans 6:23b)

Christ takes up residence inside of us-—our lives become His home.

> *Jesus replied, "Anyone who loves me will obey my teaching. My Father will love them, and we will come to them and make our home with them.* (John 14:23)

Have you ever given your life to Christ?

You can do so right now by praying something like this:

Lord Jesus, I know that I'm a sinner and fall short of God's righteous requirement. Because of my sin, I deserve death. But now I know that You love me and took my place on the cross. Your death paid for my sin. Please forgive me and come into my life. I accept You as my Savior and thank you for giving me eternal life.

If you prayed this prayer, please let me know! The angels rejoice over all who turn to Christ (Luke 15:10). I'd love to join the celebration!!

You can contact me at: https://diannethornton.com/contact-me.

about the author

Dianne Thornton is passionate for women to grow deeper in their relationship with God—the Source of Life, Love, and Truth. When you fall in love with God's Word, you experience the full, over-the-top abundant life He wants you to have. It's not an easy life, but one that is rich in meaning and fully satisfying.

Dianne is married to Tim. They reside in Pearland, Texas, and have three young adult children: Max, Rachel, and Abby. She holds a Bachelor of Business Administration degree from Baylor University.

When she has time, she enjoys long bike rides, working in her yard, and reading under the pergola she and her family built together. Occasionally, she escapes to the beach to watch morning sunrises and collect seashells.

Ways to connect with Dianne online:

- Website: diannethornton.com
- Instagram: @dianne.thornton.tx
- Facebook: facebook.com/dianne.thornton.tx
- Pinterest: pinterest.com/diannethorntontx
- Twitter: @CDiannneThornton

endnotes

[1] Spiros Zodhiates, *The Complete Word Study Dictionary: New Testament* (Chattanooga, TN: AMG Publishers, 2000).

[2] Henry T. Blackaby and Claude V. King, *Experiencing God: Knowing and Doing the Will of God* (Nashville, TN: B&H Publishing Group, 2008).

[3] Zodhiates, *Complete Word Study Dictionary: NT*.

[4] Johannes P. Louw and Eugene Albert Nida, *Greek-English Lexicon of the New Testament: Based on Semantic Domains* (New York: United Bible Societies, 1996), 675.

[5] Zodhiates, *Complete Word Study Dictionary: NT*.

[6] Charles W. Colson, *Loving God* (Grand Rapids, MI: Zondervan, 2018).

[7] Zodhiates, *Complete Word Study Dictionary: NT*.

[8] Zodhiates, *Complete Word Study Dictionary: NT*.

[9] Baker and Carpenter, *Complete Word Study Dictionary: OT*, 74.

[10] Harold W. Hoehner, "Ephesians," in *Bible Knowledge Commentary*, vol. 2, 643.

[11] John A. Martin, "Luke," in *Bible Knowledge Commentary*, vol. 2, 253.

[12] J. Ronald Blue, "Habakkuk," in *Bible Knowledge Commentary*, vol. 1, 1505.

[13] Blue, "Habakkuk," in *Bible Knowledge Commentary*, vol. 1, 1507.

[14] Zodhiates, *Complete Word Study Dictionary: NT*.

[15] Zodhiates, *Complete Word Study Dictionary: NT*.

[16] Zodhiates, *Complete Word Study Dictionary: NT*.

[17] Bill Bright, *Have You Heard of the Four Spiritual Laws?* (Orlando, FL: Bright Media Foundation, 2007).

[18] Baker and Carpenter, *Complete Word Study Dictionary: OT*, 69.

[19] Warren W. Wiersbe, *Bible Exposition Commentary*, vol. 2, 58.

[20] Baker and Carpenter, *Complete Word Study Dictionary: OT*, 481.

[21] Baker and Carpenter, *Complete Word Study Dictionary: OT*, 1171.

[22] Kay Arthur, *How to Study Your Bible* (Eugene, OR: Harvest House Publishers, 1994).

[23] Howard G. Hendricks and William D. Hendricks, *Living by the Book* (Chicago, IL: Moody Press, 1991).

www.ingramcontent.com/pod-product-compliance
Lightning Source LLC
Chambersburg PA
CBHW051148290426
44108CB00019B/2654